Never Easy...
Always Necessary

Published in the United States by
Beckham Publications Group, Inc.
P.O. Box 4066, Silver Spring, MD 20914

ISBN: 978-0-9833402-7-0

Library of Congress Control Number: 2011929999

Never Easy...
Always Necessary

Rediscovering the Ministry of Jesus Christ in an
Era of Crisis and Complacency

Rev. Dwight L. Ford

THE Beckham
PUBLICATIONS GROUP, INC.
Silver Spring

I dedicate this book to the late Paul Ford Sr., Dock Jones, and Lela Jones–a generation that resisted the soul robbery of slavery, denied Jim Crow of their dignity, and propelled our people forward in the face of indescribable opposition and odds. Ours is now a world of opportunity, because of your unfailing sacrifice to bequeath a legacy of Christian character, service, academic excellence, and pure determination to those yet unborn. Thank you for living beyond yourself and leaving a charge and challenge to become truly great.

"But he that is greatest among you shall be your servant."

—Matthew 23:11

Heirlooms to Pass and Treasures to Keep

"The Spirit of the Lord is upon me, because he hath anointed me to preach the gospel to the poor; he hath sent me to heal the brokenhearted, to preach deliverance to the captives, and recovering of sight to the blind, to set at liberty them that are bruised, to preach the acceptable year of the Lord."
—Luke 4:19

Jesus spoke these words over two thousand years ago, quoting directly from the Old Testament prophet Isaiah, yet they have an air of relevance to this present day. Tucked gently inside this scripture is an heirloom treasure of mission for the preacher that has been passed down for centuries. Although this treasure of mission was presented in a specific time to a particular audience, it has nonetheless traveled down through the centuries, being passed from generation to generation of spiritual leaders, but emerging unchanged at the advent of the twenty-first century. As a chameleon adjusts its exterior to each environment, the mission of the preacher adjusts to the outer surface of time, but the assignment is intrinsically the same in each historical context it enters. Still, the underlying mission for the preacher is to proclaim the good news: Salvation has come. This mandate to present the freely assessable "salvation" for all humanity is the driving force behind the social activism, witnessed particularly in the post-emancipation Negro church. It is evidenced in the freedom movement of the 1950s and 1960s, and remains ongoing to the present day. In a real sense, the preacher's mission of old, while traveling in and out of temples and across the dusty foot-worn highways of yesteryear, is still witnessed today by modern-day messengers, who preach the Gospel across pulpits, platforms, and on the pavement of life. The receipt of the heirloom requires that we once again proclaim, "Salvation is come" to the poor, the captive, the blind, and the oppressed of this generation.

Today, as we uncover the inherent power in the mission of the preacher, we realize and can better appreciate its true directive worth. When African-American preachers own for themselves the declaration of Jesus as a personal assignment, we become of deep and lasting value to our community, the nation, and the world. Jesus, our exemplar, preached authentic salvific hope: the expectation of eternal life through faith in God, the newness of life in Christ, and the right to cast off oppression in the here and now.

Taking ownership of this declaration means that African-American preachers must make this proclamation of salvation the heartbeat of their spiritual and social ministry. African-American history is replete with such proclamations that have proved to be the advantageous tool in our hands for breaking the chains of physical slavery, liberating our minds and souls from the abuse of Jim Crow's discriminatory laws, and second class citizenship. Our proclamation has lifted the conscience of America, holding institutions and governments accountable for the injustice and indifference in both the United States and the world. Thus, it is to all of our benefit that the twenty-first century African-American preacher continues to "proclaim good news, release, recovery, freedom, and the Lord's favor," across the available avenues of pulpits, platforms, and pavement, and do so with more vigor and vitality than ever before.

"What are those people outside waiting for?"

The significance of this mandate transitioned from theory to practice for me just over nine years ago on a warm August morning. I had recently accepted a full-time position as an associate minister at the Greater Antioch Missionary Baptist Church in Rock Island, Illinois. I was nothing less than ecstatic, overjoyed with idealism, bright-eyed, and sophomoric, as I began my ministry. It occurred on my first day, as I briskly strode across the parking lot to enter that mammoth structure of hope. I noticed a few people standing around, engaged in what I took to be casual dialogue. I dared not stop and break my professional stride, but did pause parenthetically to fling a cursory, but courteous, "Good morning." Upon reaching my destination, I eagerly swung open the heavy cherry wood doors of the century-old building with ease, sweeping through the vestibule and into the office of administration.

Behind the desk sat a smiling seasoned secretary. Little did I know at the time that her institutional memory would become a well of resource during my stay at the church. I politely informed her that outside the church, there were individuals waiting for the doors to be opened. As she did not seem overly impressed, I inquisitively, but innocently, questioned her, "What are those people outside waiting for?"

Without hesitation, she responded, "They're waiting on you."

"And what do they need?" I replied.

Her response was a laundry list of needs, "They need their lights turned on, food, and assistance."

I could not help but ask what I thought was a logical question, "Don't they have social service agencies to assist them?"

With the speed of a veteran tennis player, she returned my volley with, "The agencies send them here."

I quickly came to realize that the church, and specifically the pastor, an agent of hope and care, had earned the respect of the community. Because of the church's communal care, we eventually became the referral site for those who had burned all the social service bridges. The church was indeed a place for another chance.

Additionally, the Reverend Lance Chaney, the pastor whom I was to assist, had set high expectations for the role of the minister. In no uncertain terms, he made it clear that the minister is to serve both the congregation and the community. It was the minister's call to respond to people who are hurting, thereby becoming a defender of the oppressed and those who are voiceless. Thus, it was not unusual for me to see my pastor as community advocate, an elected official, and personally engaged in the social transformation of the community in both word and deed. This was my initiation into the social ministry.

Since that day, I have been able to combine the spiritual and social aspects of the Gospel and my life. I am sincerely grateful for the personal example found in Rev. Chaney. His love for people and his willingness to accept the community as his parish have conditioned my thinking and understanding of a pastor's call. My tenure at Greater Antioch was one of submersion—totally engulfed into church and community. I am assured that the current problems found in the human existence can be met through the agency of the church if it is fully baptized in the particular ethos of pulpits, platforms, and pavement. Such a committed church can bring a holistic understanding of what it really means to be saved, and assume the responsibility that is *Never Easy, but Always Necessary.*

CONTENTS

FOREWORD... 11

PREFACE 15

ACKNOWLEDGMENTS.. 17

INTRODUCTION: BUILDING ON A STRONG FOUNDATION..... 19

CHAPTER 1: THE MIS-EDUCATION
                    OF THE BLACk CHURCH 25

PULPITS

CHAPTER 2: BASIC EDUCATION 41

CHAPTER 3: CONFRONTING A CHRIST-LESS
                    CHRISTIANITY 54

CHAPTER 4: STICk TO THE SCRIPT 65

CHAPTER 5: THE MIS-EDUCATION OF THE PREACHER . 76

CHAPTER 6: LET GOD'S PEOPLE GO! 86

PLATFORMS

CHAPTER 7: BEYOND THE STAINED GLASS 103

CHAPTER 8: THE LEGACY OF A kING: A VOICE IN THE
POLITICAL WILDERNESS 110

CHAPTER 9: RULES OF ENGAGEMENT 116

PAVEMENT

CHAPTER 10: WORD ON THE STREET 127

CHAPTER 11: THE MINISTRY OF MALCOLM X 149

CHAPTER 12: FOR REDEMPTION'S SAkE 155

EPILOGUE

A SAVING HOPE 165

NOTES 169

BIBLIOGRAPHY 175

ABOUT THE AUTHOR 179

FOREWORD

I first met Reverend Dwight Ford on a mid-summer morning while standing on the well-traveled red brick cobblestone paths of Cambridge Massachusetts. I was a guest at the graduation chapel services of Harvard Divinity School's Summer Leadership Institute. It was there that I heard Dwight give a passionate sermon from the Old Testament book of Esther. It was an account of Esther's dilemma after learning of the impeding devastation of her people. He captured her decision-making process of mustering courage and ultimately deciding to "do something."

After the service, I made a point to introduce myself and handed my business card with these words, "I believe the movement is in good hands with young ministers like you." That was ten years ago and Dwight's Christian commitment to Christ and the most vulnerable has neither wavered nor waned. I believe that *Never Easy, Always Necessary, Rediscovering The Ministry of Jesus in an Era of Crisis and Complacency* is a book that had to be written—and more importantly, it had to be written by him.

Never Easy, Always Necessary takes a primary focus on the exemplar and chief model of ministry, Jesus Christ. Additionally, the book explores the life and ministry of the Reverend Martin Luther king, Jr. who endeavored to follow that pattern of ministry even to the point of extreme self-sacrifice and death. Dwight weaves together a pattern of biblical ministry mandates, black church history, and the life and ministry of Martin Luther king, to present a Theology of Pulpit, Platform, and Pavement.

This theology is available for further study, reflection, mediation and service. His presentation bares the evidence of careful explication of the depths of practical and public theology in prophetic and poetic tones. As one who has personally sacrificed, strategized, shared and served with the Reverend Martin Luther king, Jr. for the last ten years of his life, I was revived as I read the pages. I trust that Christians will find deep resonance, especially those who aspire towards making a serious impact on the life and times in which we live.

Dwight challenges us to rediscover the true nature of the mission of the contemporary church. He inspires the church to live out its service to God and to all people. He does so in thought-provoking and practical ways. As Daddy king, Martin Luther king's father, would often say, he has *made it plain*. And, we dare not overlook his intention in speaking lovingly and sharply to the only institution black Americans own and control, and have so, from the very beginning.

Dwight's motivation permeates the entire book. Page after page, he reminds us that the church runs the risk of failing to pass on the heritage and treasure of our God-experience to future generations. The author correctly warns us of the temptation to forsake our responsibility of leadership and service. I shudder to think of the consequences if we choose not to consider in thought and action the masses of people who currently walk in directionless darkness yet have the history of people who saw the light of tomorrow. The Good News is that a clarion call is being made through *Never Easy, Always Necessary* and many will hear once more a clear and credible word about how preceding generations in the words of the gospel song, "got over" and what we must do now to truly overcome. Those who read, understand, and absorb the pathway this book sets forth will re-discover the compass by which an oppressed people were able to withstand and overcome 400 years of bad history, while remaining among their former oppressors. Our history reveals a people with the spiritual fortitude to stand in crisis and sing a love song of Good News.

This book will delight veteran shepherds, ministers, pastors, teachers, and leaders, as well as an emerging leadership generation of apprentices, who deeply desire a clear word about how they can and must erect beloved communities of which Martin Luther king, Jr. and all our ancestors dreamed. He properly lays a theological and practical foundation upon which the visions of succeeding generations will build. For Martin Luther king and those of us who worked with him and all those who aspire to build beloved communities, this book sets forth how Jesus was and is, the chief cornerstone.

Never Easy, Always Necessary, is a call to action for those of us who have been blessed by the sacrifice of others, to work in the spirit of Mary McLeod Bethune *"lifting as we climb,"* quickening the day when bad history will meet with God's Good News. In that day, we will fully realize the ever creative ministry of Jesus Christ and renew humanity's original prospect. We long to stand in the day, which the sages saw and our fore-parents sang so triumphantly, when we "break bread together on our knees."

—Rev. Dr. Virgil A. Wood is former national executive board member of the Southern Christian Leadership Conference (SCLC) and personal friend and fellow torch bearer of the Reverend Dr. Martin Luther King, Jr.

PREFACE

"And Joshua said unto them, Pass over before the ark of the LORD your God into the midst of Jordan, and take ye up every man of you a stone upon his shoulder, according unto the number of the tribes of the children of Israel: That this may be a sign among you, that when your children ask their fathers in time to come, saying, What mean ye by these stones? Then ye shall answer them, That the waters of Jordan were cut off before the ark of the covenant of the LORD; when it passed over Jordan, the waters of Jordan were cut off: and these stones shall be for a memorial unto the children of Israel for ever."

Joshua 4:5-7

ACKNOWLEDGMENTS

I want to express my sincere and deepest appreciation to several individuals who have helped shape my Christian character, commitment to service, philosophy of ministry, and ultimately this book.

I am thankful for the undying contribution of my loving parents Dwight and Alma Ford, who have invested and sacrificed their very lives toward the betterment of our family, church, and community. Thank you to my siblings: keith Ford, Jeremiah Ford, Amber Wells, and Paul Ford for your support and contribution to my understanding of a loving family.

I am grateful for the service of several pastors who unselfishly provided opportunity for my pastoral development and have graced my life with instruction, mentoring, and wisdom. Indeed, my theological understanding and practical implementation of the Gospel of Jesus Christ can be traced to your example. Therefore, I extend sincere appreciation to Reverend James E. Lee for introducing me to Jesus Christ and for your Christian character as a leader. Thank you, Bishop Eddie J. Hooks and Co-pastor Addie Hooks, for exemplifying a pastor's heart and a committed life of prayer. Thank you, Reverend Lance Chaney, for encouraging me to pursue formal theological education, while introducing me to the mandate of church-sponsored community development and serving the *least of these*.

In addition, I am indebted to the erudite scholarship and mentoring of professors Dr. Virgil A. Wood, Dr. Preston N. Williams, and Dr. Robert M. Franklin for your personal contribution in my life through the service of the mind and by keeping the legacy of Dr. Martin Luther king, Jr. alive in your teaching and life example.

I would also like to thank those directly responsible for the completion of this work. I am grateful to the attentive eyes of my editing team: Mrs. Ruth Batton-Campbell and Amber Wells, both of whom have witnessed and worked with the earliest drafts and have polished it into a finished product. You have provided both critique and compliment. Thank you for serving as both sounding board and dialogue partners.

INTRODUCTION

BUILDING ON A STRONG FOUNDATION

"Not every one that saith unto me, Lord, Lord, shall enter into the kingdom of heaven; but he that doeth the will of my Father which is in heaven. Many will say to me in that day, Lord, Lord, have we not prophesied in thy name? and in thy name have cast out devils? and in thy name done many wonderful works? And then will I profess unto them, I never knew you: depart from me, ye that work iniquity. Therefore whosoever heareth these sayings of mine, and doeth them, I will liken him unto a wise man, which built his house upon a rock: And the rain descended, and the floods came, and the winds blew, and beat upon that house; and it fell not: for it was founded upon a rock."

Matthew 7:21-25

Looking back, I realize that my mother and father provided the foundation for my understanding of ministry. I saw my mother, a provider of early childhood education and a Parent Teacher Liaison at a poverty-stricken inner-city elementary school, serve as an agent of change and hope. I witnessed firsthand how she used her position and reputation to leverage services and resources for those most in need. Additionally, every Tuesday evening, she ministered to people, going into the housing projects and conducting Bible studies in homes and community centers. She held these studies for domestically abused women, recently released female inmates, prostitutes, drug addicts, and young teenage mothers and their children. She did this week in and week out.

Likewise, my father, a universal communicator, shared the love of Jesus throughout the neighborhood through daily interaction and redemptive intervention in the lives of everyday people: mailman, alderman, local gang members, and alcoholics and drug addicts. He was adept at affording each the dignity of being human and the hope of a new life. He possessed the quality to comfort the distressed, and with unconditional love, he challenged the daily living and decisions made by people in dire circumstances. Both parents served God, our local church, and our community with vigor, unafraid to place their lives in the paths of people, who would perhaps never attend a worship service. I am proud to say that both of them continue their ministry to this day.

Although my parents laid my foundation of service, the ministry of pulpits, platforms, and pavement was acquired later in an experiential sense through my service at the Greater Antioch Missionary Baptist Church. However, it was not until my graduate studies at Harvard Divinity School that I gained the theological and theoretical framework. I discovered a historical biblical structure and phraseology to encompass my thoughts and experience. Additionally, I was able to discern that a person and the church could embody all three expressions of ministry (pulpits, platforms, and pavement) and employ them as a whole. This was made manifest through the life and ministry of individuals like Frederick Douglass, Sojourner Truth, Harriet Tubman, and Reverdy Ransom. Malcolm X, although a Muslim, most notably demonstrated this salvific proclamation through his work in ghettos and among the formally incarcerated. His life and work deserve a rigorous mining for applicable methodologies for the present day. Without question, I have gathered the essential qualities of the ministry of pulpits, platforms, and pavement from many. However, no one person has impacted my understanding more than the Reverend Martin Luther king, Jr. Therefore, throughout this book, I will refer to the embodiment of the triad ministry in his life and legacy.

Other influences have come from my study of contemporary pastors, who utilize the power of the modern church to transform communities. Included among these pastors are men like Rev. Calvin Butts and Abyssinian Baptist Church, Rev. Charles Adams and Concord Baptist Church, Rev. James Meeks and Salem Baptist Church, Rev. kirbyjon Caldwell and Windsor Village United Methodist Church, Rev. Floyd Flake and Greater Allen African Methodist Episcopal Church, Bishop Charles Blake and West Angeles Church of God in Christ, as well as various storefront and small rural churches that work under extreme circumstances to bring hope and transformation. As one will notice, the list of my research crosses denominational lines and geography, being indicative of the fact and my belief that no one single person or denomination has a monopoly on being an agent of transformation. If authentic personal and lasting communal transformation is to occur, it must involve collective efforts from various agents and agencies of hope. In fact, my personal journey to the pulpit has included service in Pentecostal, Baptist, and Non-Denominational churches. Therefore, I hold licenses and ordinations in both Baptist and Pentecostal denominations. I learned the importance of preaching across denominational lines in Protestant chapel services as a Protestant lay reader during my six-year tenure in the Marine Corps. Therefore, I approach cross-denominational service, having gathered ecumenical principles that are also transferable across the denominational landscape. My understanding of pulpits, platforms, and pavement has been thoroughly influenced by a multiplicity of sources to include traditional and non-traditional. Thus, the definitions and typologies are a result of that understanding and experience.

The term "pulpit," for all practical and theological purposes in this book, has significance in the physical location and its theological extension. As a locality, it designates where salvific proclamation is rendered. It is fundamentally an elevated space, located in the sanctuary of churches and is set aside for sacred use. It is from this post that the preacher assumes the posture of proclamation primarily to a sectarian audience. The pulpit is in many ways symbolic and can be utilized to describe the preacher's assignment of transferring hallowed information, direction, inspiration, and meaningful utterances, in an effort to holistically develop devotees. Indeed, it is from the pulpit that theological information is rendered with the expectation of life application. The pulpit informs one's anthropological outlook and ultimately enlightens a person's sociological concern, thereby, encouraging listeners to progress, moving from theory into inspired praxis. Because the pulpit is directive discourse for life outside the sacred walls and padded pews, let us now turn our attention to the category of platforms, as a space available for implementation and action.

Unlike the pulpit, where discourse is primarily rendered to a sectarian audience, the term "platform" refers to the space from which a preacher presents a public or what I call platform theology. I base my understanding of platform theology on an interpretation of the definition by the distinguished President of Morehouse College, Dr. Robert Franklin. He defines public theology as the presentation of a person's "understanding of God, along with their ethical principles and values to the public for scrutiny, discussion, and possible acceptance."[1] This theology seeks to address the various socio-political dilemmas from a position of Christian ethics for the betterment of all humanity. Platform theologians primarily address audiences outside the confines of the stained glass and render discourse on socio-political responsibility and the lack thereof. Platform theologians engage politics and advance full citizenship from a biblical and prophetic position. As one begins to engage the political sphere, one does so with the hope of influencing public policy and raising the consciousness of the world toward those who are made invisible through indifference. Thus, the platform further presses the need for active participation on the pavement of life.

The category of "pavement" symbolizes the actual walking out of ministry, that is to say the praxis of theology in and among "the least of these" and underserved populations of the world. Pavement theology seeks to embody and employ the ethical teaching of Jesus in service to society's forgotten, the human undertow. Their very presence is an indictment to the world's lack of authentic charity and revolutionary love. Pavement theology challenges the preacher of the day to typify the redemptive work of Christ-centered action. Pavement preachers make sacrificial and unmerited love attainable and immediately accessible to all who may come in contact with them through practical and tangible methods.

In Johannine language, it is the process and realization of the "Word becoming flesh and dwelling among people."[2] This dwelling takes place among groups of the "population that do not find a comfortable place in the economic and political order,"[3] I would add, the established religious order as well. At this point, the work of criminologist Steven Spitzer is helpful.

Spitzer uses the term "social junk" to refer to people "whose lives are worn down and nearly destroyed, barely holding together. These include the mentally ill, drug addicts, lonely and frayed drifters, alcoholics, and cast-off, impoverished elders."[4]

It is not by happenstance that Jesus spent most of his earthly ministry visiting the outcasts, diseased, rejected, and downtrodden. Jesus ministered to those who were regulated to the so-called trash heaps of life. Therefore, this is the mission of the pavement theologian: transforming the human existence through acknowledgment and consideration of all. This is to say, it is an exhaustive effort through Christ-centered love to accept one as being fully human, valuable, and needed, regardless of one's external circumstantial predicament.

CHAPTER 1

THE MIS-EDUCATION OF
THE BLACk CHURCH

"If you can control a man's thinking, you don't have to worry about his actions. If you can determine what a man thinks, you don't have to worry about what he will do. If you can make a man believe that he is inferior, you don't have to compel him to seek an inferior status; he will do so without being told, and if you can make a man believe that he is justly an outcast, you don't have to order him to the back door, he will go to the back door on his own, and if there is no back door, the very nature of the man will demand that you build one."

—*Carter G. Woodson*

In 1932, the famed historian and author Carter G. Woodson published his now legendary work, *The Mis-Education of the Negro*. His book helped to revolutionize the masses of Negro people into self-determined action, to rid themselves of the psychological chains that remained on the minds of the emancipated Negro. Perhaps his greatest contribution to the struggle for freedom is found in his relentless quest to make known the lethal effects of centuries of mis-education. Woodson, challenged us to think of ourselves in a redemptive light and to cast off the yoke of mental bondage. Now, seventy-nine years later, his message is just as vital. The modern day Negro has been sheepishly led and cleverly lured back into a state of delimiting slavery. Now, well beyond the days of the rawhide whip and calloused conscience of the overseer, we face another taskmaster more insidious than cowardly and insecure slave owners.

As humanity moves through the dawn of the twenty-first century, the chains are no longer on the limbs of black bodies. Instead, they are wrapped like barbed wire around the mind. The lessons of self-hatred, self-sabotage, low-level thinking, and division were taught religiously for over four hundred years, resulting in the kind of brainwashing indoctrination that restricts the highest potential. When the mind cannot envision its highest possibilities, it becomes an agent of self-destruction, ambushing any opportunity for personal and corporate advancement. The mind under subjective ideologies and destructive theologies lies susceptible to the manipulative schemes of others. Under such an influence, we are hypnotically led into captivity by the solemn sounds of profiteering pied pipers and indifferent, self-aggrandizing parasitical so-called leaders.

Inspiration to write this book came from an intense frustration concerning the current state of the black church and the communities wherein they exist. Like the prophets of old, I weep for the liberation of my people, when I read the negative statistics that dramatically affect the majority of black people, and realize that a survey would reveal that most ill-affected black people confess to be Christians. This is not to say that I subscribe to a theology that blames those who, without any thought or action of their own, were born into homes of disarray and communal poverty. Nor do I mean to reprimand the mere existence of those nearby churches. My intention is to point to the fact that Christ is still the revolutionary liberator of, not just our souls, but our bodies as well. It is incumbent upon the church to make this proclamation a reality in people's lives.

It saddens me to think that those most traumatized live in the high crime-ridden areas of our cities and are militaristically flanked by churches on nearly every corner. In such neighborhoods, however, there appears to be a distinct disconnect between the salvific proclamation and the reality of social disenfranchisement. Therefore, one might be tempted to question whether or not the church or Christ, Himself, has lost the power of transformation. The obvious answer is a resounding and definite no! God forbid such a conclusion. For one to deny the possibilities of transformation is to deny the very essence of the Gospel. Such denials of transformation are a forsaking of the core of the mission and mandate of Jesus: to grant new life, "Therefore if any man be in Christ, he is a new creature: old things are passed away; behold all things are become new."[5] In reaffirmation of proclaimed salvation, it becomes even more important for the church to have a "hands-on" active role in transforming deprived, dysfunctional individuals and neighborhoods into healthy, productive, and self-sufficient families and communities with an increased quality of life for all.

It should be noted that the church is only one of many institutions in the community. Total transformation of our communities, however, requires involvement, collaboration, and partnership beyond the local church. The local church must work with the business sector, educational institutions, social service industry, and any organization that is sincerely committed to the betterment of human existence and the elevation of people of low estate. Additionally, the government can partner by forming non-oppressive public policies that liberate, protect, and provide a universal safety net of resources for the most vulnerable in our communities. It is no secret that many rural and inner-city neighborhoods have been strategically quarantined, due to capitalistic greed and racism.

These neighborhoods have been purposely subjected to blight with sinister similarity to that of the Tuskegee experiment. Our communities were ignored after being afflicted with the highly contagious plagues of stifling illiteracy, political weakness, fractured families, severe unemployment, drugs, predatory lending, and the cancer of hopelessness. Still, transformation is possible. The antidote lies in the power of the Gospel, which can transform hopelessness into the promised "newness of life" in our personal lives and in our communities at large. The focus must be placed on the Church, because it has proved to be the most enduring institution in the black community. Historically, the black church has been the backbone for every major initiative of social advancement for African-Americans specifically and all poor people in general. Consequently, the church, through the power of the Gospel of Jesus Christ, has the proven ability to remove the deep-rooted and institutionalized chains of modern slavery.

This book promotes a re-education of the black church on a core curriculum of liberation: priestly service to God and His people, prophetic preaching to individual and systemic injustice, godly service to humanity, and community economic development. It is a result of a persistent effort toward finding new solutions to old problems. The necessity to revisit the core curriculum stems from the fact that historically, the early black church accomplished more with less in its infancy stage than we have at the height of opportunistic socio-political and technological advantages. With Jim Crow, lynch mobs, hooded hordes, midnight marauders, mass illiteracy, stifled voter rights, in-your-face segregation, enduring racism, and blatant prejudice, the black church empowered its membership to do the impossible. It birthed schools and colleges, and contributed finances and workers in mission work to Africa without the aid of modern technology and with very meager resources. Hospitals and black businesses were funded and nurtured in its bosom. Civil rights campaigns and organizations were commonplace in many churches, and prophetic preaching was the order of the day. This is the power found in the essential elements in the core curriculum of the black church.

In an effort not to romanticize the issue, it must be admitted that not all churches were of this caliber. Status quo churches existed then, as they do today. However, it appears that a certain ethic or a sort of "in your bones" transfer failed to occur. The past speaks to the present, and in light of its history, the church today stands painfully and clearly indicted. Thus, we must ask, with all the gains, what has been lost? What has been forsaken? Has this juggernaut of justice fallen asleep at the most critical time of our history? If so, how can we reawaken her, enabling her to once again "stand in the liberty wherein Christ has made us free and be not entangled again with the yoke of bondage"?[6]

There is indeed a need for re-education: a systematic re-infusion of the core principles of the historical black church and the wisdom of application to the twenty-first century. Indeed, much has changed. Mankind has moved from the age of agriculture to industry, and finally, to the technological and information age. What remains the same is the plight of most African-Americans, both in the community, and yes, even in the Church. How long will leaders of the black church sit on the shore of perceived security and watch the masses of black people drift aimlessly in a sea of indifference, self-loathing, and low-level thinking, all the while sitting haplessly in church pews? The Church must stand at the forefront of change and remain ever so vigilant in developing each new generation to confront and face the Goliath of oppression that troubles the people of God. The Gospel of Jesus must be lived in such ways wherein, not only personal lives are changed, but also the world in which we exist. It is time for a change! The black church must embark on a program of re-education (both formally and informally) through in-depth theological analysis and intuitive life lessons.

From Whence We've Come

In the fall of 2004, I decided to take a staff position, working for St. John Missionary Baptist Church, a strong community-lifting church in Boynton Beach, Florida. At the time, I was still a graduate student at Harvard Divinity School in Cambridge, Massachusetts, and it meant that I would have to commute by plane on Thursday evenings to serve the church. It was a great opportunity, and I found it extremely hard to resist the extended summer weather, Jacuzzi-warm emerald green water, and low-hanging soft white clouds, not to mention the Atlantic Ocean breeze that has a way of dissipating a worry-filled day. It did not take long to be welcomed by the church, community, and unfortunately, Florida's hurricane season. I remember vividly the warnings as Hurricane Francis made its way toward the treasure coast. Finally, striking the coast as a category three hurricane, it brought a thunderous pounding to the placid city of Boynton Beach. As I looked out of the small porthole window in my bedroom, I was able to see the row of palm trees that were neatly lined in front of our condominium. The precisely planted trees were under the will and whim of the wind. The violence was incredible and nothing stood between the trees and the onslaught. The rampage lasted all night. In the flashing streaks of the lightning, I could see the trees that once stood so picturesque being pulverized to the fullest extent of the storm.

The morning after the storm had passed, leaving devastation in its wake. I opened the front door and saw that the palm trees that remained standing were weathered and beaten. Several of the trees were totally uprooted and lying on the green debris- filled lawn. I wondered what the difference was between the trees left standing and those that were uprooted. I noticed that all the uprooted trees had something in common: shallow roots. Without question, the determining factor of survival for the palm trees was found in a deep root system. I believe that the black church has been able to weather the storm and all its vicious enactments, because of its root system. It has a history of digging deep into the well of the strength and grace of God. We have indeed come this far by faith.

Deep Roots

As it pertains to history, the Negro church[7] was the expansion of the underground slave church. It was a church born out of the desire to be free. In a real sense, this church became a "balm in Gilead," a typology of the cultural healing ointment, expressed by the Old Testament prophet Jeremiah (Jeremiah 8:22). The prophet poetically wrote about the longing aspirations of the Israelites to be free from slavery and oppression. The Negro church appropriated Jeremiah's biblical text and applied the soothing medicine to the physical, psychological, and sociological wounds endured in slavery and oppression. Additionally, the Negro church counteracted the warped theology that was perpetrated by white Christians. The Negro church developed a theology of resistance to the oppressive and enslaving theology. To a large extent, the majority of Western Christian theology was held hostage to racist ideology that infused their concept of the world, and particularly Negro people. In short, the Bible was wrongfully and intentionally used to oppress and enslave.

Furthermore, this latter theology was instrumental in establishing laws to maintain the false sense of superiority of whites and justify slavery. Such biblical texts were utilized in this manner like Genesis 9:20-27, which is referred to as the "Hamenic Hypothesis." The emphasis was placed on verse 25, as it outlines the hypothesis: "And he said Cursed be Canaan; a servant of servants shall he be unto his brethren." This interpretation suggests that Ham, the son Noah, received a divinely-inspired curse, along with his descendants of the Canaanites, to be slaves. This wrongful appropriation becomes even more significant when one considers that the Canaanites were assumed to be black. This theology was supported by another Old Testament text, Leviticus 25:44-46. This text, through twisted interpretation, suggested that slavery was a divinely-instituted caste system and stressed the nonsensical notion that once a slave, always a slave. Thus, the theology of black subjection was used to justify colonial slavery and was supported, maintained, and projected, in large extent, by the Western Christian church.

Sadly, the role of religion was reduced to produce and justify a slave-making system of human degradation and economic exploitation. It is important to note that during slavery, a period now known as the Second Great Awakening, a move was made to convert blacks to Christianity. This move afforded soul salvation to the enslaved, but bitterly fell short of true salvation that includes physical emancipation of the Negro. The act itself, so-called evangelism, actually impoverished the Gospel of Jesus and robbed the enslaved of the salvation Jesus declared, "liberty to the captives." Jesus presented a holistic salvation: spiritual and physical, soul and body, spirit and mind—a total liberation. Anything less is not liberation, but a defacement of the liberating Word of God. So-called Christian slave owners, after the conversion of the slaves, began to use the biblical text in an attempt to promote unquestionable slave allegiance to the system that diminished their humanity and drained them of the gift of life and liberty. Again, the use of the Pauline epistle of Philemon, essentially the story about a runaway slave named Onesimus, whom Paul receives and sends back to Philemon, was utilized to dampen the hopeful flame of freedom. Additionally, other Pauline letters were used like Colossians 3:22, "Slaves obey your masters according to the flesh; not with eyeservice, as menpleasers; but in singleness of heart, fearing God." Slaves were taught that acceptance of their slave status was god-like and required dutiful service to the overseers of oppression. It was against this backdrop of misappropriated theology that the Negro church emerged to project a theology of salvation.

In time, Negro Christians began to discover the richness and liberating power of the biblical text and developed a theology with which they could identify, primarily the "Exodus motif." The enslaved Negro, having a firsthand experience of the harshest of human pain, looked naturally to the Bible for relief. In fact, when they heard the ancient story of the enslaved Israelites and Moses' prophetic confrontation summed up with the immortal words, "Let my people go," the walls of spiritual and physical slavery began to crumble. The story had a profound impact on the enslaved Africans. They began to see that God was on the side of the enslaved and the oppressed. The fact that God actually endorsed their freedom movement and voyage out of slavery gave them the spiritual strength and theological justification for resistance to any and all forms of slavery.

In addition, after emancipation, because of the persistence of racism, the Negro church was solidified as the focal point of Negro public life. It was and remains the only institution that is owned and operated with freedom from government or other systems of control. The famed scholar W.E.B. Dubois detailed the following; "The Negro church of today is the social center of Negro life in the United States, and the most characteristic expression of African character."[8] The church possessed the only assembly halls to which the black community had unrestricted access. History reveals that the "Negro church housed schools, dramatic productions, cultural events, social welfare programs, rallies and benefits of all sorts, and civil and human rights activities. By the year 1900, the Negro church impressively had compiled a remarkable record: Black Baptist associations were supporting some eighty elementary schools and eighteen academies and colleges; the African Methodist Episcopal churches were underwriting thirty-two secondary and collegiate institutions; and the smaller African Methodist Episcopal Zion denomination was supporting eight. The denomination, now named the Christian Methodist Episcopal Church, only thirty years old by 1900, had established five schools."[9]

In addition to adding value to the educational plight of blacks, the church was also the parent of black banks, insurance companies, and other businesses. The most realized benefit to society today is most likely the incubator of black leadership. Without question, the church groomed, prepared, and released intellectual and political giants. The effects are so lingering today that it is not uncommon to have a pastor who also serves as an elected public official or politically-engaged activist. The church represented the hopes and ambitions for the advancement of black people. One can only imagine the level of consideration and influence that the leaders of the church warranted. Dubois again provides a useful frame of understanding for the early Negro church and its leadership with these words: "The Negro preacher is the most unique personality developed by the Negro on American soil. A leader, a politician, an orator, a 'boss,' an intriguer, an idealist."[10] To a certain degree, the church and the preacher had the respect of the entire black community.

Thus, the Negro church was infused with both public and private interests. The term public "pertains to the associational life, and seeks to address issues of the polis broadly conceived, and engages the broad interests and concerns of citizens."[11] In reference to private, it pertains to the spiritual life and seeks to address issues of discipleship and religious service. It is precisely this dual history of the Negro church, through resistance and spiritual advancement that has led us to this place and time. Without question, this history has propelled the black church's thinking and theological formation. It must also be noted that black Christian activism, along with some of the guiding principles of the Christian social gospel, was appropriated and fused during the early civil rights movement.

Spitting out the Bones

Growing up in a family of fishermen, my palate was tempered early in life with the taste of brim, largemouth bass, and catfish. Early on, I was taught to eat fish with a few slices of white bread and a glass of milk, just in case I accidentally swallowed a bone. My parents taught my brother and me how to slowly eat the fish and digest only that which was edible. Likewise, we received adequate lessons on how to spit out the bones. In similar fashion, Christian Negroes made this technique a common practice. While digesting Jesus, the prophets, and the Gospel, they were able to set aside those dangerous aspects of the warped theology of the racist white Christians. They did it as they emerged from slavery and again a hundred years later, as the fight for freedom moved concomitantly with another theological movement: the evolution of the social gospel.

The social gospel was not delineated with authority, as a theologically distinct gospel, until the nineteenth century.

A group of white Protestant Christians in America began to examine the social ills of their day, and began to inject the social teachings and moral agency of Jesus into their context. In the late 1880s, the emerging theology came to be known as the social gospel, a theory that suggested that "Christianity would no longer be grounded in an ascetic gospel, preaching only an exclusive message of individual salvation. Rather, the church would pursue the social hope of Jesus and the primitive church to embrace the world and to transform it with a radical new message of salvation."[12] With the promotion of this new message of salvation, the proponents believed that the Gospel of Jesus Christ would "work to alleviate social, political, and economic problems."[13]

Many theologians contributed to this theology, including Washington Gladden, Josiah Strong, and Walter Rauschenbusch. Though all made considerable contributions, Rauschenbusch, "more than any other social gospel leader up to that time, wrote what amounted to a manifesto for the white Protestant middle class."[14] It is important to note that black preachers like Reverends Martin Luther king, Jr., Howard Thurman, Vernon Johns, and Mordecai Johnson, gained additional resources and theological framing of Christian social responsibility from the early proponents. However, while appropriating resources, black preachers informed and challenged the early white Protestant proponents, based on the deficiencies found in their projection. The social gospel of black theologians, pastors, and Christian activists invoked the moral strength of its adherents to address the social sin of racism and oppression with deliberate action. Early white proponents had another plan and understanding, vastly different than that of blacks.

White social gospel preachers like many white Protestants, believed that "incremental change and gradualism was the best method for implementing and achieving social justice. Their hope was based on the idea, as people were informed of the true social responsibilities enjoined by the Gospel, and acted upon them; such difficulties would yield to the active intervention of the church."[15] Because Rauschenbusch shared much of white America's paternalistic view toward African-Americans, he and other social gospelers believed that "African-Americans would be transformed by the wisdom and example of the white middle class."[16] Because of this paternalism, there would be no partnering with black Christian social activists like Mary McLeod Bethune, Reverdy Ransom, Ida B. Wells-Barnett, Nannie Helen Burroughs, and others. Sadly, the moral agency of the church, as projected by the preachers of the social gospel, granted only cursory and theoretical attention to the specificity of the race problem in America.

Thus, faced with a lack of hope for full citizenship, the abject denial of the moral agency of blacks, the high level of paternalism, and a refusal to work with contemporary black Christian social activists, black Christians began to develop a non-discriminatory theology with a moral praxis, based on the love ethic of Jesus on their behalf. Their salvific hope would become a new and distinctive brand of the social gospel that became embodied in noteworthy fashion by civil rights activists like Rosa Parks, Marian Wright Edelman, Dorothy Height, Fannie Lou Hamer, and other countless servants whose names were never recorded. Their work and service declared, in no uncertain terms, that the Gospel should make a measurable and meaningful difference in the lives of the economically exploited, politically oppressed, and socially dejected masses. Their love for God and commitment to service were manifested in their undying commitment to make appropriations from Western theologians, all the while becoming ever so efficient in "spitting out the bones."

PULPITS

CHAPTER 2

BASIC EDUCATION

"Wisdom is the principal thing; therefore get wisdom: and with all thy getting get understanding."

—*Proverbs 4:7*

It's a Matter of Respect

The basic education of the black church comes essentially from the pulpit and boils down to a simple matter of respect! That's right, respect! Perhaps the thought of such a demand from a Christian may take some by surprise. However, we are living in a day and time when the septic dregs of Darwin's "Survival of the Fittest," seem to permeate every sector of society. The survivalist ideology has stained the perception of this generation; hence, a demand of respect is necessary for the survival of the black people. Black people, now in an age of spanning social mobility and progressive education, must return to a saving respect for God. I am referring to the kind of admiration and deep appreciation that is passed down from generation to generation, like that of a precious family heirloom. What was once considered to be a sacred and treasured relationship has now become a discarded relic and void of present-day meaning.

It all happened so fast. The doors of opportunity flung open as Jericho's walls of segregation came tumbling down. The endearing relationship and respect for God were tossed aside, as we scurried across the rubbish into our Promised Land of better schools, gainful employment, and a new day of opportunity. In light of the grand opportunities, we were afforded the privilege of passing a legacy and inheritance to our children. And we did. We bequeathed unto them all the external things that make life pleasurable, and we failed to pass on to them all the things that make life purposeful: a profound respect for God, His church, and His people. In short, we have forsaken the God of our fore bearers, and have appropriated a popular culture definition of God. The Lord, for so many today, is considered to be some nameless, impersonal higher power. We rarely hear about the personal God of the Scriptures—the God our parents confidently called, "A way out of no way," "On-time God," and "My everything."

Currently, His Church is seen as a social club of good-intentioned people, who still carry archaic concepts of Heaven and hell. Quite often, in many sectors, the Church is seen as an institution devoid of power and the preacher as an unskilled, opportunistic societal nobody. The common caricature suggests that preachers are lust-crazed, dimwitted persons of failing character, with little to say to this generation. In light of this, black people must remember that history reveals that we have never advanced in promoting a good and just society without a spiritual grounding. Therefore, as a people, we must return to the basic beliefs of our fore bearers in God, and transfer a renewed level of respect for the Church. With that said, I fully understand that the Church and God's people must remain respectable. We can no longer afford unaccountable churches, pastors, or Christians. If we are to survive as a people, we must be accountable for our actions or the lack thereof, in the name of God. Respect is the result of understanding the value and worth of someone or something. Therefore, let us respect God and His work of salvation, realizing that we represent a living Savior, Christ the Lord. We have come a long way, but we have drifted off course, and our journey back will require a re- education of the principles and of the personality of God.

Not in Here!

Every Sunday in our church, children, who have been restrained throughout the worship service, are released at the sound of the benediction. They spring into the flow of the dispersing crowd with the vigor of an Olympic sprinter. Children, seeking to display their natural sprinter talent, make a mad dash across the open space in front of the church's altar and pulpit. It is often humorous to watch. As a child breaks for the dash, the parent reaches out with the long arm of the law, immediately stopping all forward motion. The parent in one motion stops movement, while simultaneously asserting the prohibitive words, "Not in here!" The parent who does this has a healthy respect for God and knows there are some places reserved for order and reverence.

The pulpit and altar of the local church are such places, regardless of how culture has influenced or hijacked the sacredness of those spaces. With that said, let me suggest that I do not subscribe to the idea that the problems of the black church stem from children running across altars and aisles in church. It is just not that simple. However, the complex and complicated issues of the mis-education of the black church quite often stem from forms of indifference and ignorance to sacred space. Many of the personal and communal challenges we face today could have been addressed in the early stages of life with such theologically reverent and simplistic phrases as, "Not in here!" Respect is the first stage of a theological understanding of God. The Old Testament prophet Moses was entreated to remove his sandals, as he stood in the presence of the Lord, because the very ground was holy. Notice that he had to give respect before he could fully come to understand the God of his salvation. In the same way, respect is the prerequisite to theological education and understanding.

As I reflect over my own childhood, I realize that it was the level of respect for God and the Church that led me to a personal relationship with Jesus. I can still remember, with great detail, the pulpit in the church of my childhood, Pentecostal Deliverance church (now Harvest Time Family Worship Center), in the river front city of Davenport, Iowa. It was, in a word, massive! It sat secure and was centrally located in the church. The pulpit was awe-inspiring to those who welcomed its presence as a sacred artifact of God. There was nothing flamboyant in its structure, possessing only an exterior of flat white paint that gently covered the hand-detailed wood-carved frame. Yet, it was both mysterious and fascinating. I was lovingly drawn to it. I longed to understand what took place when one stood behind it to proclaim the Gospel. Later, I would understand that what I had longed for could not be found in paint or wood, but in the power of the words that were spoken from that place.

In my eyes, our pulpit was as grand as Chicago's Sears Tower, standing bold and beautiful. It was humbling, for no matter one's physical height, there was something about it that required you to look up to it. When preachers of soft-spoken voices or small stature stood behind the pulpit, they were emboldened and empowered. Time and time again, I witnessed timeworn preachers become infused with strength, as they stood there. Even those, whose demeanor was generally reserved or introverted, became ignited with the fire of courage. The pulpit has a sort of cloaking power that covers our inabilities and conceals our weaknesses in Christ. Strangely, every Sunday, I saw my pastor, the Reverend James E. Lee, but I heard Jesus. It was through pulpit proclamation that I heard the voice of the Lord and decided of my own free will to make an eternal decision. On a Friday night, in worship service, I felt the call of Jesus in the preached word over that pulpit. That night, sitting next to my mother, I turned to her and passionately said, "I want to go down." I quietly rose to my feet, while the pastor prayed, and moved toward the nearest aisle to make my way down to the altar in front of that pulpit. Embracing my pastor with a gripping hug, I lifted my tear-filled eyes and voiced with my own mouth the words that changed my life, "I want to be saved."

I was twelve years old when I made that decision and walk of a lifetime. Now, as an ordained preacher, having extended hundreds of invitations, and witnessed responses much like my own, I still stand in awe of the power of God. The kind of transforming work that transpires, as we speak the Word of God, is nothing short of amazing. In our frailness behind the pulpit, we stand in God's grace, covered and concealed, allowed to communicate a Gospel that diminishes us and demonstrates His love. Although I cannot fully comprehend all that happens over the pulpit, I must say that I am so glad it does.

Power in the Pulpit

My reverential interest in the power of the pulpit did not begin on that faithful Friday night in 1982. It was groomed systematically over a period of time. A little here, a little there, it just kept growing. As a child, the embers of my spiritual curiosity were stoked every time I approached the pulpit. The most frequent opportunity came on Saturdays. Each week, my father, an ordained elder in our independent Pentecostal church, opened the doors for corporate prayer from 8:00 am to 12:00 noon. Because I loved to be with my father, I would always tag along. In that sanctuary after our prayer service, I would stand and look intently at the pulpit. Sometimes, I wondered what it would feel like to just stand behind the podium. Perhaps, if it were not for the many warnings that I received about the sacredness of that space, I would have seized the opportunity, because I possessed the kind of curiosity that would often burst into action. However, the fear and respect of the Lord had been properly instilled in me, not to mention the fear of my father! We have come a long way from that kind of respect for the altar and the pulpit as a place of consecrated service to the Body of Christ.

Sometimes, I shake my head in disbelief, as I watch the parade of clownish buffoonery that is nothing short of circus acts deemed for entertainment across our pulpits. A proper education plainly explains that the pulpit is exclusively reserved for the spiritual empowerment of people, suspended in time and drawing closer to eternity. Anything less than the spiritual empowerment of the people of God should be presented in other spaces, reserved for secular presentations. In this day of modernity, we have a responsibility to convey the sacredness of God and the spaces ordained for His presence and service.

The pulpit, for all practical purposes, has significance in its physical location, as well as its theological extension. As a location, it designates where salvific proclamation is rendered. It is fundamentally an elevated space, located in the sanctuary of churches and is set aside for sacred use. The structure can be wood or Plexiglas, massive or minute. The material does not diminish the intrinsic worth of this sacred desk. The power does not lie in the material, but in the message lifted by God's messengers. Consider the churches in developing countries, as they have limited resources and few religious fixtures, yet, the power lies in whatever space the preacher occupies. The mission and the message possess the power to sanctify any square footage for divine purposes. The space is declared sacred because the message is sacred. The power is not necessarily confined to *where*, but more so, to *what* is being communicated and to whom. It is important to note that pulpit proclamation speaks to the needs of a primarily sectarian audience. That is to say, a group of individuals who of their own volition assemble to worship, pray, participate, and receive from the preached Word of God the sustaining help and hope of this life and the life to come. The pulpit, in many ways, is symbolic and can be utilized to describe the preacher's assignment of transferring hallowed information, direction, inspiration, and meaningful utterances in the effort to holistically develop devotees. Indeed, it is from the pulpit that theological information is rendered with the expectation of life application.

The spiritual development of Christians through the teaching and preaching of the Gospel is the primary task of the preacher. Although congregational care, visitation, counseling, and public service should not be discarded, one must keep in mind that the preaching of the Word holds primacy for the preacher. It is through the preaching of the Gospel that all other forms of service are informed, validated, and even eternalized. However, modernity has critically asked, "Is the day of the sermon dead? And just how effective is the brief discourse, transpiring usually for less than one hour, one day a week?" Truly, these are valid questions and should challenge all preachers in our preparation. These questions, and many more for that matter, should serve as a penetrating and proverbial thorn in our flesh, to remind us that some person may be entering into our worship experiences as a last resort, teetering on self-destruction or damaging the lives of others. We should ask ourselves, "What does our sermon have to say to them?" We should envision the person who enters into the church as battle-fatigued, fighting to maintain his or her sanity, and struggling with the toxic stench of memories of a rape, molestation, incest, abuse, neglect, or failure.

We have more at stake on a Sunday morning or mid-week service than whether or not we "wow" people with our words or fascinate them with our framing of a sermon. There is more to be gained than a high five or a pat on the back from the choir, and expressions of how great we are from the membership. Our responsibility is to reveal the love intervention of God in humanity through the personhood of Jesus. Our preaching must relay that Christ alone can rescue us from the victimization of society and befriend our lonely souls, thus saving us from the isolation of eternity without Him. We must proclaim that one does not come to church to begin to be loved by God. When we attend church, it is an experience to reveal how God has loved us in the past, loves us in the present, and will always love us. The hymnist George C. Hugg, appropriately captured God's love intervention with the words, "there is not a friend like the lowly Jesus for all of our fears and grieves to bear."

Search and Rescue

The preached Word is the perennial tossing of an eternal lifeline to all who are drowning in life's circumstances. The Gospel reaches out to those who are vehemently treading water, searching for the security that can give them rest from their spiritual struggle and a sure foundation to stand upon. Our preaching should be more than the articulation of mere words— for in His Word alone is the life and revelation of His endless love. God searches, rescues, and transforms through His love. The love intervention of God is nothing short of a search and rescue mission, expressed weekly over the pulpit. Our reception of the Gospel has holistic implications for the complete liberation of our mind, body, and soul from the circumstances or situations that seek to drain, diminish, or threaten our total being. This assignment is a wonder in the soul of the preacher, as God utilizes failed and imperfect vessels to render a faultless Gospel to the saving of souls. Perhaps, some do not subscribe to the thought of having someone, who is in need of salvation just as any other person, be the one to instruct, direct, and inspire other lives toward Christ. They cannot grasp hinging a lifetime on a preacher's word; for them it is paternalistic at best. While for others, preaching is little more than crafted motivational speaking. They see preaching as communication, designed to intoxicate with the addictive power of a drug, formed to keep people bound in a formidable self-limiting weakness, a sort of Marxist delineation that suggests religion as the "opiate of the people."

However, those of us who have experienced the love intervention of God can verify firsthand that our faith is not found in rhetoric, but in an actual relationship with a living God. We are pursued, captivated, and ultimately apprehended by His love. We have been gripped by grace, moved by mercy, and humbled by His holiness. Those who respond to Christ are not weak or feeble-minded, but have learned the insufficiency of our state of being and God's sufficiency in elevating our "isness" into His "oughtness." The preaching of the Word of God opens our eyes and hearts to His unconditional love and forgiveness. A sermon that is rooted in the Holy Scriptures and preached by ordinary people can ignite an internal flame and provide a lifetime of illumination. One word from God can indeed change a life forever. World renowned and seasoned preacher, Rev. Gardner C. Taylor, was right when he openly declared, "How strange of God to make the uttered word, so fragile and tenuous, the principal carrier of so precious a cargo as that incalculable love which He has 'intemporated' and incarnated in Jesus Christ our Lord."[17] Preaching, unlike written communication, as longevity is concerned, is fleeting at best. However, this fleeting communication is eternally efficacious, as the Word of God lodges in the hearts and the souls of the hearers.

This charge to preach or proclaim the good news is one of profound importance, as we submit that our very lives center on the eternal exchange of projection and reception of the Word of God. If our preaching is to be authentically the Gospel, it must encompass the birth, life, death, and resurrection of Jesus of Nazareth, our salvation. It is a message that challenges who we are, while at the same time, is able to comfort us in whatever circumstance we find ourselves throughout our daily existence. The Gospel received and put into action lifts our lives to a constant striving of "becoming" Christ like. That is to say, we are admonished to depart from our dependence on detached "do-gooder" attempts to work our way heavenward and rely solely on the grace of God.

The Gospel provides, as instruction, the sacrificial example of Jesus, to counter the lessons of a superficial and materialistic societal classroom that is bent on getting more and giving less. Thus, our worship experiences demand a relative reclamation project of what was done through Christ and how it impacts our present-day possibilities through Him. It is the retelling of a familiar story that climaxes on a cross, a place where the mercy of God collides head-on with His judgment. At Calvary, a condemned world stood sentenced for the offense found in us—sin. Our substitute intervened in the affairs of the court, "For he hath made him to be sin for us, who knew no sin; that we might be made the righteousness of God in him."[18] There, on that hill, a Galilean peasant was charged only with doing "good," healing the sick, and preaching the kingdom of God. On that cross, hung a bleeding, beaten, and battered Christ, becoming, as it were, a lightning rod that attracted the thunderous judgment of a holy God for our propitiation.

This act alone brings new light to Isaiah's words, "He was smitten of God."[19] The act of the cross is not just a course in Jewish history. His action leaps from the pages and travels throughout the annals of time. He submitted Himself to dying on the cross, just to get close to us, to redeem the world, to purchase His own from sin's auction block. In doing so, He humbled Himself to a low estate, becoming as we are, to rescue us. His suffering allows Him to distinctively relate to our pain. We hold close the knowledge that, "we have not a high priest that cannot be touched with the feelings of our infirmities..."[20] Our resurrected Savior is able to comfort us because of what He endured as Jesus of Nazareth. When we feel the pain of being rejected, He comforts us through His human experience. When we suffer with the ongoing demands of leading people, He dispels our stress. When we have so-called friends to smile in our face and plot behind our back, He encourages us to remain faithful to our mission, in spite of our opposition. How can He do all of this? It is because His humanity was more than a legendary tale of a docile do-gooder. His suffering and, ultimately, His death and resurrection were done to bring us back to God. Let us never forget the Pyrrhic victory that Christ won on our behalf.

The mission of Christ subjected Him to the harshest of inhumane treatment. Therefore, firsthand experience allows Him to relate to our most vulnerable moments. The intent of Heaven was manifested in the confines of time, but has eternal and endless consequences for all humanity. His life is currently and continually expressed as the extent of a loving Savior, who brutally died and triumphantly rose again for redemption's sake. This is the power of the Gospel! It makes evident the sacrifice and provision for salvation for those who believe. These are the words that the preacher seeks to explain and exhaust within the limitations of language. Because of this, I like to say that preaching in its simplest definition is a massive translation project. The preacher, being a partaker of God's love, mercy, truth, grace, and revelation, seeks to communicate linguistically our own experience of salvation and make possible additional experiences for others to partake in the mercies of God. The corporate worship experience must contain time and place for the reading and explanation of the Scriptures, to allow others to have a God-encounter.

As one reads and embraces the Holy Scriptures through the preached Word, we dive into the reservoir of Holy encounters. Let us be mindful that God, His love through Jesus, and His power exemplified through the Holy Spirit are contained in the Scriptures. When one embraces, studies, and relays the Scriptures over that sacred space of the pulpit, one experiences afresh the love of God. Hearers are able to form and deepen a real, living, and thriving relationship with God. Imagine a God Who values His relationship with us so dearly that He chooses to speak through the Holy Scriptures. He utilizes the gift of human personality to simply amplify His loving pursuit of humanity. Because the preacher only amplifies from an existing signal of love, the translation demands that the preacher maintain a perpetual and cyclic look to the life of Jesus, as he or she relays the words of life. In all, the translations lead us all to a better understanding of our inexhaustible love relationship with God and His saving grace.

Today, we are being challenged to maintain this level of salvific concern across the pulpits in this nation. Regardless of the denominational affiliation under Christendom, geographical location, or socio-economic status of the church, there is a common threat that seeks to undermine the core principles of this glorious Gospel, so interwoven and imbedded that it challenges all who preach. This threat holds temptations with diabolical ramifications, borderline heretical, and deceitful at best. It is the lure of preaching messages that are "Christ-less" and "text-less," ultimately rendering them for all eternal purposes, "pointless." These deficiencies must be discussed in detail and an outline of diagnostic treatment prepared, to end this malignant, cancerous rampaging throughout the Body of Christ.

CHAPTER 3

CONFRONTING A CHRIST-LESS CHRISTIANITY

"For we preach not ourselves, but Christ Jesus the Lord..."
—*2 Corinthians 4:5*

As a preacher, I have been privy to hear the pinnacle of today's pulpit proclamation. Additionally, with the advent of technology and its many uses, I have studied in print and recordings some of the premier black church pulpiteers. I must confess those who have made indelible footprints upon my mental memory plates are those who have been able to reveal Jesus as being both willing and able to rescue me. From the preaching of the Word, I was able to understand that an all-powerful and all-knowing Savior understands my personal plight so intently that His care for me is not a generalized, blanketed response—a "one size fits all"—remedy. God, through the preaching of the Gospel, can address, through a sermon, the specific and precise needs found in our insufficiencies.

These preachers are able to make Christ available for the work of restoration. They inform us that Christ is available to hear us out when no one wants to listen. He is concerned with our daily struggles, and walks with us as we journey through life on earth. How valuable are the preachers, who help us form our enduring relationship with the Lord. When a preacher is able to make our risen Christ approachable, despite how low we have fallen or how far we have traveled off the beaten path, that preacher is fulfilling the purpose of the calling: reconciliation. The Christ of the Bible is the "reconciler" and the Savior of the world, "For God sent not his Son into the world to condemn the world; but that the world through him might be saved."[21]

Today, we hear less about this kind of Christ and more about achieving personal prosperity. This kind of preaching makes it easy to lose Jesus in the crowd of magnetic personalities of so many modern-day preachers. The primary goal of the preacher should always be to elevate Jesus above any one person or anything. This must become the *idée fixe* of our calling, in this age of personality preaching. It is not that I am opposed to personality-driven churches, but my concern is simply, whose personality is doing the driving.

I would like to think that John the Baptist was indeed a personality to be reckoned with. His dress was radical, his ways rustic, his personal life reclusive, and his message, deemed by the religious order of the day, reckless. He dared to speak the truth, even if it cost him his life. Nothing about him was normal. Naturally, one can suppose that his personality attracted people, if just to see or hear this overweening voice crying out in the wilderness. Yet, John built a powerful following, trained and tutored many in the way, and introduced the Sacrifice of God on the muddy banks of the Jordan River, declaring, "Behold the Lamb of God which taketh away the sin of the world."[22] However, John, with his highly explosive personality, gracefully bowed before the Lamb when Jesus assumed His public ministry, stating, "He must increase, but I must decrease."[23] What a proclamation from the premier preacher of his day! He possessed an infectious personality, but was humble enough to recognize that Jesus is the only star, for salvation is indeed of the Lord and only through the Lamb of God. Likewise, today our personalities are not the problem; it is the placing of them under Christ that becomes the major challenge of today.

We must restrain our egos in a Church culture that helps to feed our base desire to be praised, exalted, and served. The rock-star receptions on our behalf, the celebrity status we enjoy, and hypersensitive aloofness, generated by our protective custodian escorts, can distance us from the people we love and seek to serve. We cease to feel their touch and no longer relate to their day-to-day struggles. This kind of distracting attention is exclusively centered upon selfish glory-grabbing desires and not upon the One who has been, is, and will be forevermore. The current pop culture of clergy is heavily saturated in supercilious man-centered madness. It is a magnet for foolishness and it is at the core of the detachment between pulpit and pew. We are challenged to promote Jesus, as we wrestle with a changing model of leadership that requires face and name recognition in a market-driven society. Ours is the work of ensuring that people will come into contact with Jesus and not just our books, products, or conferences. Our goal is that in all things Christ is glorified through our much-intended and needed contact with people.

The earthly ministry of Jesus was an ongoing assignment to reveal the love of God through His service. It was daily, tedious, and God-centered. This He did beyond the Sabbath, as He willfully intervened in the affairs of people. Christ willingly shared not only His preaching, but also His time with people. How far have we drifted from Christ's example? Today, the higher the elevation of the preacher in terms of title affiliation (bishop, denominational president, apostle, or prophet), the less time we have to develop disciples daily. This is the reality of the institutionalized Church. Lest we forget, we have both the responsibility to preach and pastor. The ministry of Jesus was mobile, more like that of a traveling evangelist and not restricted to weekly services in the same location. We have the mandate to preach the Gospel to all and the pastoral call to make disciples, which is a day-in and day-out process. The question becomes, how do we accomplish this, while constantly seeking ways to preach the Gospel to the entire world?

To begin with, we must ensure that our titles or denominational affiliated positions enable us to attain our corporate goal of preaching Jesus, rather than our becoming enslaved to the position. Next, some us are appropriating new twenty-first century mega-church paradigms in our churches without differentiating the size between what we refer to as the mega-church and the traditional church size of seventy-five to one hundred and fifty persons that is attended by the vast majority of Americans. The leadership of a mega-church may in some ways be equated to that of a mayor, as the congregation may be the size of a small city with a budget to match. This is not to suggest that the leadership of such churches should solely spend the bulk of their limited time in counseling sessions or visitations. Understandably, distinct emphasis is often placed on the "business management" of the mega-church, more than on the more inclusive pastoral duties. On the other hand, leading such large congregations does not exempt one from pastoral leadership duties that are biblical and essential to making disciples.

It is my belief that every preacher should do a reasonable share of counseling and pastoral care. It is a labor of love to serve the membership in this manner. Avoidance of the shepherd's responsibility to dwell or walk alongside the people robs the preacher of the insightful tender touches of God's grace being activated in the daily lives of the people. When we miss this, we tend not to reflect the love of Jesus, the Good Shepherd. When Jesus is not premier in our ministries, we tend to overlook our priestly duties of sacrifice and service. Jesus, having been with the people, relates to all He encounters. The book of Hebrews informs us that He was "like as we are tempted in all points, yet without sin."[24] The reason He can relate to us is because He was both like as we are and with us.

American Idols: The Seduction of Celebrity Status

A failure to focus on Jesus produces a congregation and a people that are easily attracted to and ensnared by self- centeredness. I will never forget a very interesting young man whom I met during my third year as a Master of Divinity student at Harvard University. Although a first-year student, he seemed quite sincere and had little trepidation when he asked for my assistance in finding a church in which he might preach, while attending school. I invited him to lunch to learn more about him, in order to assist him in his endeavors. Having built a good reputation as a liaison between the school and local church community, I knew of several churches. Over lunch at a restaurant in Harvard Square, I asked, "In what areas would you like to serve?"

He responded almost flippantly, "I don't want to serve, I just want to preach." Regretfully, I informed him that I could not in good faith help him if he was disinterested in serving in some capacity, wishing only to roll in on Sundays to preach a weekly detached sermon.
I admonished him to reconsider his thoughts about service, because the churches in which I fellowshipped were seeking servant-leaders. He was not deterred in the least. He politely thanked me for the time and stated, "I will

find a place." Sadly, within a matter of weeks, I received joyous word from him stating, "I found a place."

What a disservice to the Body of Christ! Here, a young preacher, in the midst of forming his understanding about Jesus and his personal calling, exhibited no interest in service to a local congregation. Unfortunately, this is far too common among many seminarians, who, because of a few classes on the history of the Bible, hermeneutics, homiletics, analysis of the Scriptures, or the experience of having preached a handful of quotation-filled, packaged sermons in the safety of their colleagues or home churches, have a tendency to sell themselves to local congregations as having arrived. They enter the ministry thinking that they have little to learn from the local congregation, but with everything to teach them, as a result of their recently acquired scholarship. They render research without relationship, which more often than not is received by congregants as lofty platitudes, having little to do with the present pain of people. Only an informed agent, serving and ministering, can make a meaningful application of the academy in the congregation. Service and preaching are connected in concatenation. We offer lasting contributions through our Christ-centered service, just as Jesus came not to be served, but to serve. And the greatest among us is the servant of all, not just in the service of preaching, but in life.

Image Is Everything?

I am the first to praise the developments in Christian television. Today, more and more pastors and churches are purchasing time on major prime time and cable networks. Long past are the days of the pioneers like television evangelists Billy Graham, Jim and Tammy Baker, and Jimmy Swaggart. Today, African-American pastors are making their mark in television. Currently, they are the new face of the televangelist. A major difference between the pioneers and the present-day television preachers is the fact that the pioneers were essentially evangelists, that is to say, preachers of the Gospel of Jesus Christ, by and large without the pastoral responsibility of a congregation. In stark contrast, today's so-called televangelists are primarily pastors. In fact, they are the pastors of mega-churches: congregations of two thousand or more members. The one thing that has remained the same for many television preachers is the solicitation of money, and perhaps, in today's setting, an overly punctilio emphasis. Still, it is not the over-emphasis of money alone that I am concerned with. Rather, it is the images that are influencing, above any other demographic, young preachers, and would-be pastors. The captivating influence among this demographic fundamentally arises from the presentation of a roseate image of success, rather than service.

Click to any channel where televangelists are on, and the far too frequent image will be one of expensive designer suits and Italian-made alligator shoes. In light of the obvious, it would nonetheless be petty and non-germane for me to base a critique solely on the personal selectivity of the preacher's attire. My point here is to direct attention to a *prima facie* image as a total package of so-called success and little to no inference on the responsibility of service. The problem occurs when one takes the clothing in combination with the luxury cars, ever-expanding salary packages, and the ever-present entourage that closely resembles a fanatical frenzy of "gospel groupies" who pamper and answer every beckoning call in the name of service. Most disturbing about this image is that the pastor is catered to in non-biblical and inscrutable ways. What one ingests is a not so subtle inference that preaching is about personal prosperity and this thought is just as injurious as suggesting that service is a vow to personal poverty. Both are non-scriptural and developed through interpretations that are misleading at best. Cable television is both the blessing and the bane of this generation. We now have the power to reach millions across the airwaves with the Gospel of Jesus Christ. Yet, the gift of salvation is often wrapped in the mis-educating imagery of preachers, as being the recipient of service, rather than the chief servant in the house of God.

There is an onus of responsibility to train and educate the next generation of would-be preachers in the necessity and benefits of godly service. When we elevate young preachers to the pulpit without first helping them to develop a servant spirit, we create within preachers a mindset that service is what everyone else should do. Sadly, immature preachers assume that service is something that should be provided for them. To develop a minister without a servant heart is Frankensteinish and horror-filled, a deadly philosophy indeed. One who espouses such a philosophy is but a manufactured, pieced-together clone of a preacher, devoid of authentic human compassion and consideration.

Furthermore, this spiritually-barren philosophy becomes manifested in sermonic content, and thereby, reveals the preacher as uniformed. The uninformed preacher has little to no contact with the people he or she has been called to serve through the various struggles of a life laden with disasters, unachieved aspirations, and other critical life situations. The lack of information, acquired through pastoral service, detracts from the experiential understanding of the good news of Jesus Christ. Additionally, one can become a disillusioned ecclesiastical elitist, in the sense that one can actually come to demand the graces that a membership can sincerely bestow upon a pastor.

Today, the issue is not the service of the people, but the service of the pastor, leaving one to wonder whether pastors really understand the day-to-day frustrations of the everyday working people, who are unable to take a day off with impunity. These are the people, who labor to be at church throughout the week for Bible study and to serve in a variety of volunteer ministries to meet the needs of the congregation and community. In time, the "servant-less" preacher becomes spoiled, pouty, and condescending to the membership, when they fail to attend one of the service offerings or go through personal spells of drudgery. How we respond to such realities is indicative of lessons learned through the vested time with people.

Pastors must remember that a great portion of the pastoral responsibility is to lead people to a closer relationship with Christ. Therefore, to accomplish this, we must know the people to whom we preach. Preaching is more than throwing out a few properly-placed phrases, catchy one-liners, and intelligent delineations. Becoming a truly great preacher requires time spent in and among the people, sharing tragedy, as well as triumph, smiles, and tears. For the sake of learning, life demands pastoral participation beyond the Sunday worship experience and the preaching moment. Thus, the preacher must be committed to becoming a student of the people he or she serves through the Word and through pastoral responsibilities.

We Preach Jesus

The Gospel, lacking the underpinning of Jesus, will ultimately fail in offering salvation. The New Testament book of the Acts of the Apostles strikingly details the events of the first Church, giving special attention to that band of believers. The disciples, who were chosen, led, taught, and empowered by Jesus in the Synoptic Gospels, are mobilized by the Holy Spirit in the book of Acts. The empowering of the Holy Spirit mobilized and transformed the disciples into what is truly known as apostles: "sent ones" for the promulgation of the Gospel of Jesus. The writer, St. Luke, grants us a glimpse into their hopes, as the fourth chapter of the book of Acts unfolds. The apostles, having experienced the outpouring of the Holy Spirit in the upper room, activate their faith on the streets, performing signs and wonders. The great stir created by preaching disrupted the ritualistic existence of the Roman occupied citizenry, so much so, that the local religious authorities sought to rein them in. The authorities recognized that this new religious movement was threatening the established status quo. As a result, the religious hegemony weighed in with a vengeance, despite the fact that they were not forming a movement against Judaism. The apostles, nonetheless, refused to be bound by Jewish ritual law. Being neither devotees of the Greek gods nor a part of the cult of the Emperor Caesar, they operated wholly under the auspices of what society deemed a failed political ideology, derived from a social outcast and a peripheral nobody, in comparison to that great city, Rome. The apostles were agents of Jesus the Christ!

The proponents of Jesus have no intellectual acumen that the Greeks should value. They have no theological sanction or rabbinical rights that the Jewish leaders should honor. The apostles had no social power that Rome should respect. Although they had none of the attributes needed to be a respected sect, there was one fascinating, even mysterious attraction. According to the Scriptures, "they [rulers, elders, and scribes] took knowledge of them, that they had been with Jesus."[25] Their boldness and demeanor were a reflection of the light and life of Jesus, so much so, that in later chapters of the Bible, they would be called "Christians" because of their Christ like service and stand. It is no wonder the followers of Christ in the first century Church were willing to die before they would denounce the name of Jesus, "For there is none other name under heaven given among men, whereby we must be saved."[26]

Yes, we preach Jesus. But if preachers are truly to preach Christ, they must be equally assiduous in practicing service, as we are in preaching. It becomes necessary, then, to return to Christ-centered sermons that are more than Sunday morning motivational talks and polite pontifications about how to become successful in business or improve one's social standing, which by today's definition constitutes spiritual peace. Instead, the preaching of Jesus challenges the sin in our lives and comforts the spiritual longing of the soul to be fully and consistently reconciled to our Savior. Jesus did not come simply to give us a relative peace. He came to give us eternal peace with God, which is the internal understanding of Christ as our Savior. Therefore, the very presence of Christ in our lives alone brings internal peace. Externally, Jesus, on our behalf, confronts the agents of discord and dissolves the infectious envy and fear that stifle the hearts of people through our daily service.

As a child, I heard the familiar closings of preachers, who whooped, rhythmically ending sermons the same way, Sunday after Sunday, by going to the cross, in picturesque fashion, they captured the climactic calamity on Calvary's hill. They would roar the pain felt on the cross and groan the death of the Savior by dramatically dropping their heads below their shoulders. Finally, they would start the countdown of how many days He spent in the grave, ultimately raising their voice to make it known to all: "Early on that third morning, He rose from the grave!" By that time, the entire house would be standing. I really did not understand how the people could get so happy about something they heard every Sunday. It was not a new story. Actually, it was the same old story! What I did not know then, but am acutely aware of today, is that though the story is the same, the experience of the Savior is ever renewed. For in this story is the constant reaffirmation of salvation through one Savior, the God-man, Jesus the Christ.

CHAPTER 4

STICk TO THE SCRIPT

"For we preach not ourselves, but Christ Jesus the Lord; and ourselves your servants for Jesus' sake."
—*2 Corinthians 4:5*

"All Scripture is given by inspiration of God, and is profitable for doctrine, for reproof, for correction, for instruction in righteousness: that the man of God may be perfect, thoroughly furnished unto all good works."
—*2 Timothy 3:17*

In the dense forest of eastern North Carolina, on a humid August evening, I stood in full combat gear with my platoon, as a student in the Marine Corps School of Infantry. We were beginning a training operation and I had been assigned as the navigator. Confidently gripping my compass and assured of my ability, I walked toward the platoon sergeant. I was ready to roll.

I had the map to plot our course and the compass to determine our direction. The platoon sergeant smiled, as I approached. He grunted out a command to "put that thing up!" I can still remember his words, "I don't need a compass to get to our location, I know these woods." Respectfully, I asked, "Are you sure?" Again, he squalled, "Put that thing up and follow me." "Well," I thought to myself, "He does this all the time; I will just follow his lead."

Off we went into the green monster. It was not long into the patrol before we realized we were off course. We had neither reached our predetermined location to set up an ambush nor had we any way of determining our present location. To further complicate matters, a heavy blanket of Carolina night began to crawl across the graying sky. We were indeed lost and in the worse way. In the increasing darkness, we wandered around in circles, holding the belt loops of the person in front of us, because it was too dark to see the person immediately before you. Six hours later, following the "pop-up flares," sent out by our company in search of us, we stumbled into camp physically drained, mentally exhausted, and shamefully battered by the jeers of our fellow Marines.

That experience taught me that even an experienced person can drift off course. The Lord saw fit to leave us the Holy writ to guide us into salvation and a meaningful relationship with Him and humanity. Jesus, our exemplar, left an example for all pulpit preachers to follow. After He received the open confirmation of the Father in the murky Jordan River, as that great forerunner John the Baptizer publicly baptized him, Jesus, under the direction of the Holy Spirit, departs into the wilderness for the private consecration of fasting and prayer. It is in this season of personal sanctification that Jesus becomes the subject of severe testing and temptation from the adversary.

Thus, those who are called to public ministry should expect nothing less than external and internal testing and temptations, as we draw closer to the purpose of the Gospel of our Christ. It is in the seasons of personal consecration that one learns the intense lessons of self-denial, total dependence, and ultimately, experiences the victory of the Lord Jesus. Christ understood this and submitted Himself as the target for the enemy's spiritual and mental affliction. Throughout it all, however, Jesus withstood the onslaught by victoriously resisting the enemy with the missive Word of God. He responded to each of the devil's temptations with, "It is written." Jesus used the written Word in His season of testing and it was essential in His victory over the enemy. How much more should we follow the example of our Savior?

Lifestyles of the Talented and Text-less Preacher

The question of the day is, "Why do we have a surge of contemporary preachers, who are drifting toward a text-less preaching, when we have Jesus as our example?" Perhaps, this rush of text-less preaching is spurred on by an effort to better relate to the daily lives of the people. Because research into the practices of modern-day Christians and non-Christians tends to illustrate how few people read the Bible, text-less preaching may be an attempt to down-size Scripture to a level easily comprehensible to Christians and the masses untutored in biblical study. I am the first to admit that relevance is important and certainly one should use wisdom in reaching those who do not have a relationship with Jesus, as it pertains to the Holy Scripture. At the same time, I am able to sympathize with a world turned off by religion gone awry, where many prefer seeing a sermon in action than hearing one. Nonetheless, it is extremely dangerous for preachers, no matter how seasoned or well versed, to attempt to articulate a message of their own, devoid of scriptural reference. The surety of salvation found in our mandate is to faithfully serve as translators. However, we are on the verge of ushering in a day of scripted, quip-filled, golden-tongued monologues that are devoid of the insightful exposition of the Holy Scripture. There must be a return to a relationship with the Word of God as the only map, the *vade mecum*, compass, and tour guide on earth.

It is not enough to suggest a return to scriptural preaching without a few words of caution. In the last twenty years, we have seen a change in the type of clergy responding to the call of God. In many ways, the shift broadened the religious *tête-à-tête* to include non-traditional strands of black people. In light of the positive, I must say that the transitions were in many ways needed. Thus, I am most appreciative. However, in an effort to counteract the negative aspects of tradition, some have negated a very important and required process of mentorship, training, and basic theological education. This is not an indictment of non-seminary educated preachers, for the Lord is no respecter of persons, and He will use whom He will to preach His Gospel. In fact, I started preaching long before my official ordination and seminary degree. Thus, I know firsthand that the seminary does not validate the authenticity of a person's call, neither does one attend seminary to discover Jesus. Without question, one must have a personal conviction and experience with the living Savior before attending any seminary or Bible college. I count myself to be extremely graced and privileged to be included in the vast number of mentored and seminary-educated preachers.

However, because many preachers have developed a tailored and very effective ministry without seminary or formal training, it is assumed to be a dispensable luxury. In fact, there is an impression that the pastorate is one of the most accessible, I dare say, non-investigated vocations available to the unlettered. Since formal training is not a general prerequisite, one does not have to explicate or present an apologia before formal boards before starting a church. It is not customary that congregations question at length those who claim to be called to preach and pastor. So, for many, preaching becomes nothing more than a thirty-minute inspirational talk with sort of a shotgun approach that flings a few verses of scripture into the air, while listing a few points of interest to keep the momentum building, and portraying a deep and spiritual disposition. But preaching is more than finding a few scriptures to back an opinionated slant concerning life. And pastoring is more than having a flexible work schedule and comfortable office. The preacher has the responsibility to employ the gift of preaching to shape and prepare individuals for quality living on earth and an eternity with Christ.

It's in the Approach

The hermeneutic approach to preaching suggests consideration be given to how the Scriptures are interpreted. What are we looking for when we examine the text? Is it sermonic content, denomination affirmation, or truth? The manner in which we approach the Scriptures will determine "what" we will say. Be mindful that one who has the best intentions can approach the Scriptures in a vertiginous manner, wherein the result can be the genesis of serious misinterpretations. Proper interpretation is akin to piloting a plane. Consider a plane in flight for example. Before the pilot can successfully land at the intended destination, there are a number of required actions that must take place, no matter how well-intentioned the pilot may be. First, the plane must descend to the proper altitude, and proper adjustments made, as the plane is positioned to approach the runway. If the approach is wrong, the result can be disastrous. In like manner, preaching has to have a systematic and proper approach to land properly in the hearts and minds of people. There are three initial checkpoints to credible biblical interpretation: historical analysis, contextual consideration, and proper application to the daily lives of the people for practical implementation. The challenge of the preacher is to allow this process to occur. Yet, the message must be spoken through the distinct personality of the preacher without clouding the atmosphere of the preaching moment with cataract distortions of personality and personal experiences.

How Do You Read the Scriptures?

It is important to note that the human mind processes information through the lens of personal experiences. Our experiences in the past, whether positive or negative, help to determine how we read Scripture and what we count dear in the text. For instance, if one comes from a very legalistic church background, one tends to count the Pauline epistles dear, because they enforce doctrinal beliefs. "Wherefore come out from among them, and be ye separate, saith the Lord, and touch not the unclean thing; and I will receive you"[27] can take on regulatory sanction against attending football games, movie theaters, and bowling alleys, or enforce clothing restrictions and such. If one has the experience of a more liberal church formation where parties, alcohol, and pre-martial sex were familial discourses and not pulpit directives, then one tends to avoid the Pauline corrective letters and focus on the issues of justice and institutional sin, rather than personal sin. Therefore, we first seek to apply the promise of the Scriptures in our own life. For example, the approach that a former felon may take upon a scripture like, "If the Son therefore shall make you free, you shall be free indeed,"[28] can solidify a lifetime of assurance in the face of a judgmental society. What I am suggesting is that our experiences assist us in determining what is meaningful to our relationship with Christ. Although Scripture must be interpreted through experiences, that interpretation must also go beyond our personal experience to include the inspiration of God, inherent in His Holy Word. Therefore, to gather the right interpretation, one has to consider the historical contextual analysis of the scripture being expounded upon. Because we preach from selected passages of Scripture, or a pericope, the text we preach is connected to a pre-text—the scriptures before our selected text—and a post text—the scriptures that follow our text. To get the full meaning of the preached text, we have to take all three components into account, in order to gain an accurate contextual understanding. Also, one cannot ignore the fact that the Scriptures were written to address the specific circumstances of that time and period. That is not to say that the Bible does not address the times in which we live, God forbid such a conclusion! We must, however, take into account the historicity and align that with the present situation. Not to do so can lead to inaccurate interpretation and application.

Proper Application

A few years ago, I lived in Florida. Upon arrival, I soon discovered that Tampa has seasons where the pollen atmospheric levels are extremely high. At those times, I sometimes suffered from sinus irritation that led to a painful sinus headache. In an effort to relieve a pounding sinus headache, I normally sought specific pain medication. As you know, there are many types of pain medications on pharmacy shelves, addressing everything from headaches to backaches. Although backache medicine may address pain in general, it could not meet the specific need of my sinus headache. The specificity of the pain drives one to apply medication with precision. Just as I sought to apply the appropriate medication for my headache, the same specificity of selection is needed to ease the pain of the soul. Whereas, the text-less preacher depends on a general call to God's healing medicine, a preacher with the knowledge of Scripture can apply the healing ointment of God through proper interpretation and application of the Word. Exemplary is the pain of miscommunication caused by pejorative language. A healthy dose of the medicine from the Book of James can address with precision the issue of proper communication. Likewise, if one understands that the context of the Apostle Paul's letter to the church at Philippi was used to reassure the people in the face of trials and tribulations, Paul's letter might also be used to offer spiritual solace to someone whose thoughts of financial insufficiency make them fear that they lack the ability to make a difference in the lives of others. One can, in fact, make a major difference with minor resources through Christ Jesus our Lord. The specific scripture, "I can do all things through Christ which strengthens me,"[29] provides the base for this thought. A historical and contextual view of this text will reveal that Paul was encouraging the believers in Philippi, in their attempts to financially support the Apostle. Although the church at Philippi could not be as benevolent as they intended, Paul informs the church that he has learned how to remain spiritually stable with or without financial security. However, in that they gave with pure intentions, the Lord affirms through this letter that small acts can change the course of a person's life. Additionally, Paul teaches us through his lack that one should never delimit their ability to serve God and humanity because of financial need.

This is not to say that a law school student cannot quote the same scripture in preparation for the bar exam. A man struggling with an addiction to pornography can also quote this scripture in his moment of temptation. Herein lies the expansiveness of the Scriptures. No one person or circumstance is excluded from the benefit of a selected or singular scripture. The Word of God is effectual, advantageous, and meaningful to those who have a personal relationship with God. No degree or historical backdrop is needed to communicate with a risen Savior, who loves us unconditionally.

Here is one final example, to draw this point to a conclusion. A contemporary and controversial issue revolves around women in ministry and positions of leadership in the Church. The common critique about women in ministry and leadership is taken from the words of the Apostle Paul. In consideration of Paul's admonishment, "Let your women keep silence in the churches: for it is not permitted unto them to speak, but they are commanded to be under obedience as also saith the law. If they want to learn anything, let them ask their husbands at home; for it is a shame for women to speak in the church."[30] I suggest this scripture should be taken in context with pre-text and post-text included, considering the historical setting and Paul's reason for writing it in this letter to the Corinthians. Let us start by stating that Paul is arguably one of the most liberating writers of the New Testament. His declarations include such ethnic and gender affirmations as, "There is neither Jew nor Greek, bond nor free, there is neither male nor female: for ye are all one in Christ."[31] In further consideration of Paul's letter and command to the women in the Corinthian church, we are challenged by the thought that the apostle is addressing specific problems of confusion and disturbance, caused by a particular group of women attending the church at Corinth. Thus, in an effort to silence the constant quarreling, it is feasible to conclude that this letter was meant to specifically address the problem at hand. It should also be noted that Paul, in correcting via written communication, might have been inclusive of "all women" in writing, rather than explicitly naming those involved. Any leader will attest that quarrels are best handled up front and personally. Finally, we are reminded that the Apostle Paul was a man of his day, a leader in a patriarchal society. Yet, his calling to expand the Gospel and level the playing field of salvation for all shields him from hasty convictions of demonstrating improvident disdain for women in the ministry.

A proper presentation of the Gospel takes more than a microphone, a polished speaker, and a tailor-made suit. It takes a desire to study and grasp the full understanding of what is being said, as well as what is not being said in the scripture. We strive to present the wisdom of the Scriptures that may be concealed by language or obscured by history. The task of the preacher is to sift through the language and historical barriers and reveal the gems of the Gospel.

A Gold Mine

The preaching of the Gospel of Jesus Christ requires an understanding of the "what" we say or hermeneutics, as well as a fundamental understanding of homiletics, the "how" we say what we say. That is to say, on Sunday morning or whenever we mount the pulpit and stand behind that sacred desk to deliver, "Thus says the Lord," we will be involved in either *exegesis* or *isogesis*. Exegesis is the process of extracting information from the text. In simple terms, it is letting the text speak without the superimposing of secular sources, ideals, precepts, and such to gain meaning. It is uncovering what is already there. I am convinced now more than ever that much of what is declared as, "Thus says the Lord" is actually, "Thus say I." The truth of the matter is that the power of preaching is in the Word, not so much in the delivery, though I believe delivery is important. I have heard preachers fumble through the English language, unlearned and unlettered, yet they maintained a single focus on the text and not themselves, so that at the conclusion, Jesus was realized in salvation. The power is in the Word, not our style, whether we are structured sophisticates, down-home whoopers, trained teachers, or simply struggling to find our own voice in a sea of influences. The strength of transformation is in His Word. God will indeed speak through us, if we allow the Word of God to preach to His people.

Does the Bible Say That?

On the opposite side of the preaching discipline lies *isogesis*, the process of reading into the text. I feel that this method presents two foremost challenges to the preacher. First, it becomes very easy to drift into our self-promotions of ideologies that may or may not line up with the Word of God. Second, one can surmise independent doctrinal truth. I have had the experience with isolated churches that declare independent truth that is distant from the Body of Christ. They end up with private revelations and develop presumptuous church-wide fanfaronade arrogance, as if they are the only ones who are going to Heaven. This is the result of reading into the Scriptures man-made doctrines that separate and divide the Body of Christ.

Reflecting on this section, I know that preachers involved in ministry may not be able to stop and attend seminary or bible college, because of monetary challenges and time constraints. If that is the case, it is of the utmost importance to develop consistent and in-depth study habits and acquire bibliographical resources that can aid one in the understanding and delivery of the Gospel. The Bible is God's gift to us. In a very real sense, our lives are based on the direction contained within the boundaries of the sixty-six canonized books. So, let us study, prepare, and diligently work to ultimately become, in my words, "text-nitions," trained to dissect and deliver the Word of God with precision and passion.

CHAPTER 5

THE MIS-EDUCATION OF THE PREACHER

"Any religion which professes to be concerned with the souls of men and is not concerned with the slums that damn them, the economic conditions that strangle them, and the social conditions that cripple them, is a dry-as-dust religion."
—Rev. Dr. Martin Luther King, Jr.

Kings and Kingdoms

There is a grave deficiency found in the modern preaching of the kingdom of God. It is manifested in the extreme polarization between poverty and prosperity. With the recent growth of mega-churches in the African-American community, great attention is being paid to the pastors and the message of prosperity being expressed across pulpits. Neither large churches nor prosperity preaching is novelty in and among

African-American churches. However, the notoriety and the influence can now extend far beyond the local neighborhood or city scope. The use of technology and television has taken the message global. Some investigation reveals that the charismatic and evangelical strand of the universal Church has utilized technology far more than the rest of the Body of Christ. In fact, it is interesting to note that many of the forerunners of prosperity preaching were independent or non-denominational churches. Today, many of our preachers possess a newfound independence, church growth, personal wealth, relative influence, and power. Thus, they operate in a more autonomous fashion, outside denominational boundaries. Essentially, the doctrine, decisions, and determinations of these pastors are decentralized at the local church level.

In this day of freedom, senior pastors of autonomous or independent congregations must take proper precautions in ensuring that the freedom of independence does not equate to unaccountability. Every pastor, denominational or non-denominational, should have systems of accountability for the sake of the Gospel. The answerability and liability of the preacher are becoming a lost concept in the twenty-first century. Perhaps, the decline in denominational power has tempered the surge of independence among pastors. One of the noted benefits of church autonomy is that pastors have the freedom to expose their perspective congregations to different denominations and various preachers, and promote fellowship that stretches beyond denominational alliances. It is safe today to suggest that, by and large, we are becoming more committed to and concerned with kingdom building or ecumenical fellowship than denomination building.

However, the emphasis on the kingdom has done more than foster cross-denominational fellowship. It has infused our desire to build massive structures with campus life realities. Our acquisition of stretching acreage, multimillion-dollar worship centers, family life centers for recreation and the promotion of the arts, private educational facilities, and entrepreneurial business ventures bespeaks our ability to become sufficient unto ourselves. The building of such can be a glorious praise to the goodness of the Lord, as He has allowed a multiplicity of services and opportunities to be centralized for the sake of the people of God. However, there are a few warnings that should be issued, as we seek to establish the kingdom that Christ preached.

The kingdom motif without question is the most commonly preached among the non-denominational mega-churches, although it is not totally exclusive to these churches or to large memberships. One reason for the familiar jargon expressed in larger churches is that it is easier to draw comparisons to the kingdom motif if there is a realized sense of a realm of people, resources, and interests to govern. The question of how to govern the blessings of human and social capital is an immense challenge. Much of what we understand about kingdoms is based on the imagery of the Old Testament, particularly in the examples found in Israel and king David. In such, there can be found proven principles of governing. However, with historicity, the imperative of contextual application demands a proper employment of the timeless model and principles. Old Testament kings lived in natural or physical realms. In the New Testament, we see the hopes and longings of another kingdom coming to earth. Christ Jesus unveiled a kingdom, not of brick or mortar, but of justice and righteousness—a realm ushered in by the Spirit of God.

The preaching of the kingdom is not new. Actually, it was the basis of all that Jesus preached. Time after time, Jesus taught His disciples and the masses what the kingdom of Heaven or the kingdom of God was like. There is no need to differentiate between the kingdom of Heaven and the kingdom of God. Both delineations are essentially the same thematic proclamation, concerning the ordered life of the citizens of the "Spiritual kingdom," with the mandate for continual praying for the manifestation: "Thy kingdom come, thy will be done on earth as it is in heaven."[32] Therefore, the phraseology should not intimidate us, for salvation commits us to the work of ensuring that righteousness and justice are extended to all.

The challenge we face is not in the phrase, but in relaying a proper interpretation and appropriation of the kingdom. First, let us realize that the kingdom of God cannot be built. It is not a location that we can quarantine off with impenetrable gates, to protect some utopian existence on manicured lawns with overly polite greeters and parking lot attendants. The kingdom is a set of God-instituted principles for daily living that supersedes all earthly wisdom and logic. It is a system where righteousness is validated through our relationship with God. That is to say, a person is considered righteous through the blood certification of Jesus. Faith in Jesus Christ is the birth certificate that determines one's citizenry in the kingdom. Therefore, it is not of works or deeds that one is made righteous, but by faith alone. kingdom citizenship, however, does not end with a God-to-humanity relationship, but includes a God-through-humanity relationship as well. God-to-humanity is the work of the cross, while a God-through-humanity is the realized resurrection in Christ Jesus for the sake of reconciliation. The Scriptures have declared, "Therefore, if any man be in Christ he is a new creation."[33] The newness of life is expressed in how we treat each other. In other words, just acts or even better, justice, is a result of kingdom citizenry. We are considered just in relation to how we relate to others. If one is kind, fair, considerate, compassionate, judges well, merciful, and loving, then one is truly just. In a real sense, the kingdom that Christ preached could not be built, but rather was brought into existence through His devout obedience to the Lord, even unto death, which instituted a radical love ethic that brought Heaven to earth.

It seems by mere observation that kingdom building in the twenty-first century is not unlike that employed by the Old Testament kings. Let us keep in mind that the word "kingdom" denotes that there is both a positioned and physical king. Unfortunately, our model of kingdom leans more to that of an earthly realm, rather than an eternal one. Furthermore, we tend to hinge all things spiritual on the leadership of a physical king. I am fully aware of the order of leadership, having served six years as a United States Marine and as an Associate Pastor for five churches. It is both a necessity and a privilege. Yet, processes for establishing a just society can become stanched in fatuous hierarchies, which does little to serve God and His people.

Certainly, one should respect and honor the positioned leadership of the church. However, positional leadership should never eclipse the radiant authority of Christ. The Apostle Paul affirms this by saying, "The head of the church is Christ."[34] Therefore, it is vital for us to understand that historical kings, although godly at times, were neither prophets nor priests. Their position was not greater or less than; it was in a category of its own. The dispensation of legal power was vastly different for kings than for priests. The last word of a king could determine whether a person lived or died. A king, in a rudimentary understanding, was a totalitarian for the sake of the kingdom. The appropriation of Old Testament king models by servant-leaders may explain some of the dictatorship expressed in some of our churches, whether denominationally or non-denominationally affiliated.

When we subscribe to totalitarianism, we are essentially suggesting that the king is beyond all earthly accountability. After all, who is the king accountable to but God? It is true that our churches have boards of elders, deacons, ministers, stewards, and trustees, all of whom are charged with assisting and providing accountability. However, such groups serve as puppet coalitions for tax purposes and are considered devoid of any real power of exacting accountability. Many boards have become an assembly of well-dressed manikins. My critique of non-accountable leaders does not suggest in any way that I am in favor of a democratically-governed ministry, where the political vote runs and rules the direction of the church. A pastor must possess visionary discretion and the power to lead the congregation without politicking for the popular vote. My comments are more toward cases of congregational abuse through unrestrained pastoral freedom and the use of absolute power that Lord Acton appropriately warns us "absolutely corrupts."

A recent review of articles capturing the scandals of the abuse of power, fiscal mismanagement, and sexual misconduct, reveals that many of my fellow clergy had at their disposal boards of accountability and sadly some of the boards were fully aware of and even participated in the moral decline of the pastor. One brief biblical example of this sort of mutual unaccountability can be found in the story of king David. Let us consider the number of aides, attendants, or servants who could have possessed first-hand knowledge of his adulterous affair with Bathsheba. But who could have intervened with the affairs of a king? In fact, it took a prophet to confront king David, while his staff and attendants were impotent to challenge his behavior. When kings go off-course and enter into sinful behavior, there must be a prophet: a person who can speak truth to power, while maintaining a concern for God's elect, but without fear of consequence. The courage to hold people of power accountable with respect and reverence is a rarity today.

Those who serve in the capacity of a prophet operate in a spirit of righteousness and justice. Often, good pastors with godly intentions serve in hostile environments between the pastor and boards. In such situations, many have moved to dismantle boards of accountability, in order to evade constant confrontation under ungodly board tyranny. This may be understandable, but it is neither biblical nor wise. Such action makes it easy to handpick a few people with unquestionable allegiance—people who lack the godly responsibility of tactfully and respectfully pointing out potential character pitfalls along the way. There must be a mutual respect for positions and the differentiation of power and responsibility. The members of boards or deacon ministries are not there to handcuff the pastor, confine creativity, or strong-arm the direction of the church. They are there to uphold ministerial vision, administration, and service, in an effort to strengthen the abilities of the pastor and support the overall leadership decisions of the set leader.

The Old Testament reveals the elders' ability to assist Moses in the counseling of the congregation. The elders were men of nobility among the people. Likewise, the role of Moses' ministers was to hold up the arms of a tired pastor, as he stood praying on behalf of the people. Likewise, the deacons found in the New Testament were called to serve and assist in the care of the congregation. Notice, none of the aforementioned suggests that neither elders in the Old Testament nor deacons in the New Testament were called to dictate the direction of the church or the pastor. Never should there be a power struggle in the Lord's church! God has positioned a pastor and if that pastor has not maliciously led, manipulated the church, or spiritually sinned against God, then those who serve God and His church should stand with and behind the set pastor, even in the face of disagreement. There is nothing more toxic than ministers, deacons, or elders seeking to divide the church or sway the vote for fear of losing power or because of an outright unwillingness to let the pastor lead. It is ungodly, and I dare say, satanic! We must re-educate our congregations biblically, not just denominationally, on the role of ministers, deacons, and lay leadership. Finally, pastors are not to exact leadership as an earthly king, but as a part of the spiritual lineage of the king of all kings, He who led by serving and was exalted because He humbled Himself. I love to preach about David and the godly kings of Israel. However, let us remain aware of the limitations of their positions and our appropriations of power.

A King's Complex

An in-depth look into the book of 1 Samuel will reveal God's thoughts concerning the concept of king leadership over His people. It was at a time when the prophet Samuel had served Israel with dignity and honor. However, the same cannot be said about his two sons, whom he appointed. The sons of Samuel were deceitful in making judgments and took bribes. In light of this, the elders deduced that they wanted to be as other nations with a king to rule. The Lord's response bespeaks both a warning and an understanding of the intricate and interwoven challenges that are inherent to the position.

"Now therefore hearken unto their voice: howbeit yet protest solemnly unto them, and show them the manner of the king that shall rule over them. And Samuel told all the words of the Lord unto the people that asked of him a king. And he said, this will be the manner of the king that shall reign over you: He will **take your** sons, and appoint them for **himself**, for **his** chariots, and to be **his** horsemen; and some shall run before **his** chariots. And he will appoint him captains over thousands, and captains over fifties; and will set them to ear **his** ground and to reap **his** harvest, and to make **his** instruments of war, and **his** instruments of **his** chariots. And he will **take your** daughters to be confectionaries, and to be cooks, and to be bakers. And he will **take your** fields, and your vineyards, and your olive yards, even the best of them, and **give them** to **his** servants. And he will **take** a tenth of your seed and of your vineyards, and give to his officers, and to his servants. And he will **take your** menservants, and your maidservants, and your goodliest young men, and your asses, and put them to his work. He will **take** the tenth of your sheep: and ye shall be **his** servants. And ye shall cry out in that day because of your king which ye shall have chosen you; and the Lord will not hear you in that day. "

I Samuel 8:9-18

A closer look will reveal that the position itself tends to be self-serving. Notice, if you will, common themes in this text. First, consider the word "take." It is neither negotiable nor debatable. The king acquires from another, and it is interesting that the taking does not only occur from conquering nations, but the taking, as God warns, is from within and among the people of God. Notice again, the complete phrase, "He will take from you." What is deemed important for the king and the advancement of the kingdom is acquired. The Lord realized that the temptation in the position to serve the people and be ruler over them is often too much for even the anointed of the Lord. Let us not forget that Samuel did anoint with oil, and that the Lord allowed Saul to serve in this capacity, for he was the man whom the people desired. But every earthly king has the potentiality of possessing a destructive complex.

The king model of pastoring threatens the fabric of congregational care. A king has to dominate, and exact decrees and orders to be obeyed. If orders are to be obeyed, the king appoints others to ensure that orders are carried out. The slightest notions of disobedience will bring immediate and harsh consequences, because if the thought goes out that the king can be denied, the infrastructure will implode upon itself. Unquestionable loyalty is essential for this model. For this reason, many who carry this complex have dissolved deacon boards, eliminated elder councils, and any public sessions where the people can ask the senior pastor questions concerning direction or purpose. The king model is one where the people are not consulted for input and are kept in the dark, yet their dollars and service are required for advancement.

I want to make one point painfully clear. I do not support the rule of the people in the Lord's church. Any such implementation is not biblical, for the ultimate accountability belongs to the leader. I lift this challenge of leadership to reveal how pastors can impact a congregation in ways that are oppressive. The goal of the pastor is to strike a balance between undeniable vision and directed leadership without denying adherents the right to either question or give appropriate input. Any system of governance that does not operate in a spirit of consideration makes of willing servants into mummified followers and ignorant slaves.

CHAPTER 6

LET GOD'S PEOPLE GO!

*"And the LORD spake unto Moses, Go unto Pharaoh, and say
unto him, Thus saith the LORD, let my people go, that they
may serve me."*

—Exodus 8:1

Saved to Serve

Several different Greek words are used in the New
Testament to capture the meaning of servant. There is *diakonos*,
where one serves of his own free will, usually without pay and
for the benefit of others. Next, there is *oiketes*, where one is
held accountable for the master's household possessions, in
the sense of a steward. Additionally, the word *misthotos* is used
and is indicative of one being hired for service. Then, there is
the word *doulos*, which is found commonly among the Pauline
epistles. It is actually the word for slave: one who is brought
under the domination of another, so much so that the will of
the master is superimposed upon the person. When Paul uses

this word, he is suggesting that he is the slave of God, and his total will is that of the Father. His labor is fully concentrated toward the fulfilling of the desires of the Lord. The word is one that Christians can relate to without trepidation, as it pertains to the Father. But when the word is used to describe the same position in reference to serving another person, it can evoke abuse in the worst way.

The major difference between service and slavery in the church is that in service, we want people to submit to the direction and leadership of the church, because this brings about a healthy harmony, to achieve unified goals and preserve the order needed in the organization. As a servant, I subjugate my own will for personal and collective benefit, and in so doing, I grow in the graces of the Lord and exemplify my Savior, Jesus. However, when I become a slave to another person, I am dominated in ways that are not productive for my personal growth in Christ. I become thingified—a breathing tool to accomplish the drives and ambitions of another. The text previously quoted (I Samuel 8:9-18) warned the Israelites that kings would become domineering, allowing their personal agenda to overshadow all others. When people are taken for granted, used for personal gain, and positioned for politics, the masses are led into a distorted sanctified slavery. The enslavement is deepened by preachers who twist theology, proclaiming that the blessings of God rest in whether or not congregants personally serve the pastor, and suggesting a special anointing reserved for those who, without question and without limits, serve their pastor.

The pastor must resist this urge to promote self as the sole agent capable of giving or passing on the anointing. I have even heard preachers say, "If I am to give my anointing..." as if to say, "I can dangle something over the head of the people, and for them to get what I have, they have to be to me what I need." If the anointing comes from God, then how does it become solely ours to give? We may share contacts, influence, positions, advancements, even promotions, but the call and anointing are ultimately from the Lord. Let us recall Samuel, as he went to the house of Jesse to anoint a king. Remember the oil did not flow for anyone except he whom the Lord had appointed. When we suggest that we are the repositories of the anointing, we engage in mordant madness, seated in our arrogant and distorted understanding of the call of God.

Called to Conquer or Serve?

Under the Old Testament, the Lord allowed the advancement of a people and the conquering of societies deemed ungodly. king David was without question the greatest king of Israel. He expanded the kingdom more than any other king during the united existence of Israel and after the regional separation of the nation. Because kings are called to conquer, they are naturally privy to the spoil, riches, and wealth of the conquered. Pastors who follow this model are bound to pursue monetary gains. However, that is not to say that pastors should not receive salaries that are comparable to the secular professional world. The Bible distinctively states, "Thou should not muzzle the ox that treadeth out the corn. And the labourer is worthy of his reward."[35] On the other side of the coin, God calls the preacher to minister with or without financial provision. In the Synoptic Gospels, Jesus sends His disciples out to preach, informing them to take nothing for their journey: no money, no food, or other resources deemed necessary. The question that every preacher must ask is, "Would I do this if there were no monetary gain?" The preacher, if truly called by God, has to preach for the saving of his or her own soul, and must give an account to God for the souls he or she serves.

Still, I am an advocate for the just increases and equity of clergy salary packages. Far too many do not respect the time, education, and experience many pastors bring to their service. However, because of the intense debates between clergy and boards over financial packages, some pastors have taken a more kingly approach and seek to gain equity and additional opportunity for financial security. On one hand, this occurs legally with the formation of private ministries, usually formed under the preacher's name or initials with the word "ministries" attached. I take no negative stand on such endeavors to broaden ministerial opportunity and financial security. My intention is to bring to light some of the crass economic-driven initiatives that plague the Church. On the other hand, we must fend off the temptation to hold million-dollar anniversaries or the ungodly lifting of offerings in worship for private gain.

As a preacher, I understand that the offering is an essential part of worship, and my responsibility is to remind people of the commands and promises of the Lord concerning how to give, both joyfully and liberally. This in turn reminds the congregants of how Christ freely gave all for us. The reception results in a joyful and liberal return of God's graces. Yet, the almost strong-arm tactics being used today are little more than thuggish Sunday stick-ups and manipulative pandering for personal motives. A distinct line has to be drawn between manipulation and ministerial encouragement. If it is manipulation, the gain is private, and if it is ministerial, the gain will be corporate. God does reward the giver, but it is based on the heart of the person, not the size of the gift. And we should never require a certain amount before praying earnestly for individuals. I believe money lines and special prayers given to the highest givers do not reflect the Spirit of God, for He is no respecter of persons. If the heart of the five-dollar giver is in right standing with God and the heart of the person with the five-thousand-dollar gift is far from God, He will respond based on the relationship of heart and not the amount of the gift.

Another challenge presented by the king model of pastoral leadership is maintenance. Once a territory is acquired through war or by other means, it has to be protected. Representatives are sent in to set up societal infrastructures, to maintain order and protect the interests of the invading agents, at the expense of the conquered community. The interests are at the kingdom level, not the communal level. That is why the Lord warned Israel not to desire a king, for they would lord over the people in oppressive ways. God was not interested in a monarchy, but a theocracy, where He ruled the people. We have in Christ, a divine king, who provides a model that lifts the low, defends the weak, and maintains order through the power of love.

Divine Kingdoms and Decaying Communities

In recent years, a great number of African-American churches have become increasingly more astute in financial prowess and budgetary concerns. With this new opportunity, some have ventured out from their urban centers and headed for the Promised Land of suburban landscapes. The expansion and acquisitions often result from their current lack of available space to expand facilities or services for growing memberships. At other times, the migration can be attributed to a belief that the move out of the inner city is a long-awaited promotion from what we called in the Marine Corps, "hardship duty." This type of migration may be seen as escapism, the attempt to avoid the conflict between the church and the community.

For those who remain, that conflict has led to gated fences, state-of-the-art alarm systems, and the employment of security guards inside and outside the sanctuary for both church and pastoral safety. Countless inner city church parking lots are flanked with uniformed visible deterrents. The employment of this type of necessary action can cause a contradiction of belief, as the safest place in the community is only safe due, in part, to armed agents, prepared to protect the people and the property. Theologian Reinhold Niehbur brings light to this thought by stating, "Christians may feel compelled to undertake actions that are less ideal, even tragic, for the sake of preventing the greater evil. These actions grant the strength to deal with inner city realism."[36] In other words, the kingdom must be protected, and understandability so.

Observing recent trends of church migration forces us to consider the negative effects upon the community where the exodus transpires, the new community into which the church enters, and the effects upon the church itself. Many relocated churches over a period of time consciously or subconsciously lose touch with the neighborhoods that are in dire need of a representative voice for righteousness and justice. Thus, relocations can create a greater gulf or disconnect between the church and communities that are in desperate need of the prophetic voice and witness of the church. Surprisingly, the disconnection is also becoming a critical concern with churches that remain in urban centers. The need to safeguard person and property often hinders any interaction between those inside the gates with those outside the gates. The people within the gates often fear those on the outside, while those on the outside distrust and despise those on the inside. The mandate of Christ challenges us, out of reconciliatory necessity, to place our focus on serving God above all, as we labor to bridge the gap between the two groups.

The lack of pastoral influence in the local community may also stem from the "no-to-slow" leadership transition inherent in churches. Normally, in the Old Testament king model, monarchs died in office. Sadly, too often, in the church leadership, transition only occurs in death or because of serious illness.

More significantly, however, many of the long-standing church leaders often become limited in vision and fall into the trap of seeing the community and the people as a hurdle in the way of advancing the kingdom of God. This mentality demonizes the surrounding area of the church and presents an "us-versus-them" theology. This result is primarily because the leader and congregation have a substantial history with the community, and it may unconsciously limit the possibilities of spiritual and physical salvation for those who are geographically closest to the church. It becomes painfully obvious, as sermons escape the topic of neighborhood transformation through service and committed concern, for those outside the church walls. In the absence of such concepts of service, walls of inner sanctification and outer damnation are erected. When this happens, the leader and the congregation can become desensitized, similar to that of a homicide or crime unit, approaching a murder scene. Professionally, as a part of their work, they may have viewed the carnage of many crime scenes in the past. Consequently, as a result of their work, they may fail to feel the significance of the individual departure of human life and what that lifeless body represents to others.

The life and work of the urban black pastor is to touch the heart of people through the love of Jesus. What makes the mandate complicated is that, in time, calluses can grow upon the pastor's ministerial hand for the protection of the serving agent. The calluses actually allow one to continue in service and survive the many different pains of inner city ministry, but the side effects produce a preacher's hand of ministry that has become non-responsive to the sensitive areas, requiring a tender heart and hand of ministry. The antidote to desensitized leaders and congregations is to establish a system of renewal that reflects upon the graces of God in their own individual lives. In reflection, one is renewed with the realization that God sent Jesus to rescue the most undesirable, rejected, cold, and distant persons, which includes all of us and those who live in the communities we serve.

Making the Connection

The disconnection, even discord, between kingdom and community is an issue that requires an exposition of methods to bridge gaps. Certainly, the church will operate under the kingdom authority of God, but that does not mean it operates in total disdain for the community in which the church exists. However, let us be mindful that the disconnection can also take place inside the church walls. Sometimes, the kingdom is divided internally. As I stated earlier, churches are becoming more mobile than ever before. The reality of mobility changes the demographics of the local church drastically. Today, church membership does not necessarily reflect the community in which the church is located. It is not uncommon to find members who travel between thirty and forty minutes to attend worship services. This was common in rural areas, but is a recent occurrence in the urban centers. The effect of the commuter church expands the ever-increasing present-day gap between members and unified memberships. When the membership is not reflective of the community in which it resides, the church must establish connections through service and commitment to the area and its people.

...Divided We Fall

The undesirable ways of social distinction has invaded the Church. The classism that we abhor in secular society has crept into the most sacred of places in an insidious way. Preachers must work extremely hard to reduce the divide between the haves and the have-nots, the educated and the illiterate, the strong and the weak, in the confines of the sanctuary. The

Church cannot afford to allow its worship experience to become a one-dimensional service of self-gratifying and pompous back-patting for the popular and prosperous. God has called the preacher to minister and the Church to be an edifying and elevating space of love and appreciation for all.

The New Testament book of James reveals a congregation that demonstrates how this disconnect can exist in the most sacred of spaces. The idea of favoritism or partiality threatened the Apostle James and the Jewish Diaspora that he led. He asks,

"My brethren, have not the faith of our Lord Jesus Christ, the Lord of glory, with the respect of persons. For if there come unto your assembly a man with a gold ring, in goodly apparel, and there come in also a poor man in vile raiment; and ye have respect to him that weareth the gay clothing, and say unto him, Sit thou here in a good place; and say to the poor, Stand thou here, or sit here under my footstool: are ye not then partial in yourselves, and are become judges of evil thoughts? ...If ye fulfill the royal law according to the Scripture, Thou shalt love the neighbor as thyself, ye do well: but if ye have respect to persons, ye commit sin, and are convinced of the law as transgressors."

James 2:1-4,8,9

James is writing to a congregation, where Christ is declared to be central, yet social class systems have swept in and produced an ecclesiastical imbalance in the treatment of the members. Special privilege was given on the premise of appearance, dress, and societal position. Far too often, clergy can become so intoxicated with the thought of high standing or wealthy persons attending worship services that they cater to them in ungodly ways. Never should a person be granted leadership positions in church simply because of his or her position in society. Just because a person is a professor at a local college does not necessarily mean he or she should be a Sunday school teacher or a Bible study leader. Likewise, if a person is an accountant in a law firm, that does not warrant his or her immediate access into the church fiscal department. With that said, the church should look for both competent and capable individuals who exemplify Christ like character with a significant level of professionalism. Likewise, a person who is anointed or has sacred duty in worship services is not necessarily qualified to balance the church budget. All leaders in the church should be evaluated, based upon their Christian character, experience, calling, and expertise, and never based upon socio-economic status. In Christ, there should exist a freedom from the prejudices and discriminatory actions of organizational structures and persons in secular society.

The pastoral responsibility of ensuring the congregation feels connected to each other is real, to say the least. If a bond does not exist or is unrealized, the Body of Christ stumbles in epileptic jerks and the unity of Christian movement is disturbed. In times of adversity, people will not stand together unless they feel the love and concern of others. This is why members of congregations heavily populated the protest marches during the civil rights era. The connection had been made and was tested in times of personal and collective crises. Thus, people were willing to stand together, walk together, and suffer together, in hopes that they would be saved together. In a spirit of reconciliation, we should strive, not only to bring people together, but also to bind them together in unified action.

Pulpit Priest: A Living Sacrifice

The reconciliatory work of the pastor has been expressed in countless preachers, but I have come to appreciate the great sacrifice and service of Rev. Dr. Martin Luther king, Jr. When one listens to the sermons of king, one discovers the concept of salvation. For king, salvation is concerned with both the spiritual or the eternal destination of one's soul and equally concerned with the earthly deliverance of one's natural body. The goal of salvation is based on the mission of Jesus, "For the Son of man is come to seek and to save that which was lost."[37] king, rather than detracting from this scripture, built upon the foundation of Jesus with salvific preaching outlined in Luke 4:17-19. This scripture text is recorded as one continuous thought of rescue, redemption, and recovery. It is my assertion that the flowing thought derived from Jesus is that salvation is holistic and paramount to every Christian truly concerned about the destiny of people.

The preacher must stand in agreement with Jesus, as salvation is to include the spiritual, economic, social, and physical deliverance of persons. In actual terms, salvation is inclusive of every segment of one's life. In this case, Dr. Robert Franklin is helpful, as he specifically addresses the concept of holistic salvation. "The best of the black church tradition focuses steadily on both the personal and social transformation. It emphasizes that personal conversion, moral renewal, and sanctification should manifest themselves in acts of justice, charity, and service in the wider world."[38] What king envisioned was a unified body of civilization that universally renders love in the service of restoration, justice, and reconciliation. If we are to embrace reconciliation, we must realistically address the societal ills that fracture the hope of restorative justice.

king proposed restorative justice as a means to reconcile whites and blacks. He frequently criticized the polarized preaching of his time that emphasized only a salvation in Heaven. This imbalanced gospel was and remains an impoverisher of the possibilities of a present salvation and fatally encourages listeners to hang on until a better day of liberating death. In his final speech, delivered over a pulpit, he released a seasoned rebuke with these words.

It's alright to talk about 'long white robes over yonder,' in all of its symbolism. But ultimately, people want some suits and dresses and shoes to wear down here. It's all right to talk about 'streets flowing with milk and honey,' but God has commanded us to be concerned about the slums down here, and his children who can't eat three square meals a day. It's alright to talk about the new Jerusalem, but one day, God's preacher must talk about the new New York, the new Atlanta, the new Philadelphia, the new Los Angeles, the new Memphis, Tennessee.[39]

His critique was based on the economic injustices that prevented the unity found in reconciliation. However, restoration ensures that all represented are emphatically free. For king, it was not enough to stand holding hands singing, "We shall overcome" with whites, if upon the conclusion of singing, blacks went back to the confines of poverty and whites to the vastness of possibilities. Restoration considers injustice and seeks to replenish that which has been depleted, to make reconciliation a probability.

A Royal Priesthood

As priest, the preacher faithfully offers the Gospel with two overarching themes: reconciliation through love and redemption through the cross. The preacher must take the role of priest with grave sincerity. It is a journey where we are called to walk with people, as they make their way back to God. The long walk back is guided by love. Now, when I refer to love, I do so primarily referring to the Greek word, *agape*: the sacrificial, unconditional, and non-discriminatory action toward and on behalf of others. This kind of love is not based on the possibility of reciprocity. Rather, it flows from the giver's teleological goal of reconciliation. The end itself is a right relationship with God and humanity. I have come to greatly appreciate the words of Dr. king, as he defined love in the following manner.

Love is not meekness without muscle. Love is not sentimentality without spine. Love is not a tender heart without a tough mind. While it is none of that, it does mean caring. Love means going to any length to restore the broken community. Love means going the second mile to restore the broken community. Love means turning the other cheek to restore community.[40]

In this reference, the term *broken community* is emphasized. The broken community is the opposite realization to what king commonly referred to as the *beloved community*. This beloved community is based on justice and concern for the *neighbor*, which is perhaps most akin to a Lukan concept of the kingdom of God, where love is rendered to the *least of these*. Only the power of unconditional love can hold society together and allow us to stand before a Holy God. The work of Christ was to first draw us closer to God and empower us to draw closer to one another.

It is the priest, who remains available to serve humanity in a fragmented society. The root of our fracture is not found in racism, classism, genderism, or any other "ism," but it rests in "sin." It is our sinful heart that separates us and dims our vision of seeing the best in others. I am aware that some may consider the concept of personal sin to be solely an evangelical notion. And others will consider the breaking of commandments and non-acceptance of Jesus' blood sacrifice on Calvary for our sins to be an outdated Flintstonian and archaic belief. Nonetheless, I am persuaded that if we dealt with the sin issue, we would witness a decline in the persisting problems that have plagued our existence. Lest we forget, sin not only separates humanity from God, sin is also the separator of humanity. I will speak more of this separation in a later chapter.

Due to the existence of sin, reconciliation in the Judeo-Christian faith demands a sacrifice. Once again, the Old Testament speaks to us, providing the historical account of God covering Adam and Eve with the skin of innocent animals. These crescendos in the New Testament crucifixion of an innocent Jesus, not just to cover humanity, but also to cleanse us from all unrighteousness. The thought of the innocent suffering for the guilty was expressed in king's commonly quoted short phrase, "Unearned suffering is redemptive." The life of the Christian preacher is one of sacrifice—a rendering of our total being for the sake of reconciliation.

Embracing the Cross: All Will Give Some, but Only Some Will Give All

The cross is a symbolic connection to the life of Jesus. king understood the necessity to connect with Christ through suffering. It should be noted that king, based on his education, could have very easily enjoyed a middle-class lifestyle in secular career fields. However, he yielded to the cause of Christ and to preaching the Gospel. His cross was wrapped in his care for humanity. He freely offered his life as a sacrifice for the freedom of the oppressed and the redemption of the oppressor, stating, "The cross is something you ultimately die upon."

king, as a preacher of the Gospel, was fully aware that the cross, both of historic and symbolic significance, has but one purpose and it is summed up in the word, "death." The cross for the Christian is indeed a place of death, but never defeat. The cross was not the end of the story for Jesus and it is not the end for us. Our theology is one that includes both death and resurrection. We must embrace a theology of death and resurrection in all its theoretical underpinning and make it practical, in the sense that our suffering for others leads to communal care. Suffering itself is a kind of death. The concern for others is the process of emptying oneself of selfish drives, greed, and lust. Yet, in the process of voiding these negatives, one is lifted to a higher standard of life, thus being resurrected by the power of God.

In the analysis of the cross, we are made aware of the radical love that Jesus displayed. This love is to be expressed, not only outside the church, but inside as well. Our lives rendered in suffering are reconciliatory and salvific. Thus, in concluding this section on the pulpit ministry, the preacher's role as a priest, and the goal of reconciliation through love, special note is taken of the fact that sacrificial love transcends religious denominations and envisions the world as one extended body of civilization from the common denominator of Adam and Eve. The preacher should promote a belief in the connectedness of humanity and the aspirations of a world at peace in word and deed. The theme of love has to saturate our sermons and drench our daily lives, as we dutifully function as priests, bringing people back to God. Our role should emphasize evangelism in the traditional sense, as well as a revolutionary love that calls men and women to consider their neighbor, regardless of the expressed differences of our religious beliefs. Therefore, we are encouraged to love others, to fulfill God's desire for community, and to serve as the priests of old, bringing humanity's sin and sacrifice to the altar, where the all-powerful blood of Jesus can make us whole again.

PLATFORMS

CHAPTER 7

BEYOND THE STAINED GLASS

"Your people will rebuild the ancient ruins and will raise up the age old foundations; you will be called the repairer of broken walls, restorer of streets with dwellings."
—Isaiah 58:12

It was a Wednesday, and I had a full-day schedule with meetings and appointments. As I darted in and out of the Tampa lunch-hour traffic, I thought of the short speech I would deliver as the co-chair of the University Area Community Center Faith-Based Coalition at our year-end lunch meeting. I parked the car much like a professional stunt car driver, while whipping out my cell phone to confirm the time of my next appointment. I wrapped up my phone call, while simultaneously walking into the meeting room. In doing so, I felt as though I had entered an ambush. I saw the co-chair standing, fending off a bombardment of questions. Immediately dropping my bags, I moved to stand next to him, and the barrage of questions quickly shifted to me. I listened intently to a bright and zealous young man, as he asked, "How serious are churches about the community. We never see them outside their churches. Pastors should be on the street like Jesus." In response, I assured him that his critique was warranted and welcomed. "The church," I said, "could do more in areas of utilizing their facilities beyond Wednesday night Bible study and Sunday worship services. In fact, we have the ownership of our buildings and should seek ways to better the community through the use thereof— whether in the offering of GED classes, workshops, mentoring programs, or other empowering opportunities."

The more I took ownership of the lack of communal support and spoke respectfully concerning the intentions of the coalition, I could feel his level of cynicism dissipate, at least for the time being. At the end of the dialogue, I pointed out that the Church is one institution among many in the community with the mandate to make life better for all. The schools, businesses, hospitals, and local government, and yes, the local church must collaborate as partners to solve the problems of the community. The Church is the kind of institution that can serve public interests and remain private. It has the distinct purpose of being a religious institution, comprised of religious people who live in a very public world. Therefore, to impact the totality of a person, whether Christian or not, preachers must venture outside the church walls in service, and their discourse must venture well beyond the pulpit.

The preacher and the church that makes a public impact have taken seriously to what I call the platform. This is essentially the space outside the four walls of the sanctuary or religious medium. In this space, preachers serve as public theologians: people who offer their belief in God to a secular audience. As a public theologian, the preacher freely displays the religious and ethical teachings of his belief for the public to embrace or reject. Platform ministry occurs in public spaces. It happens in secular media, prisons, assembly halls, and other venues not solely defined as sacred. It is from these spaces that we declare a public theology, "the engagement of a living religious tradition with its public environment—the economic, political, and cultural spheres of our common life."[41]

The platform has been a part of African-American proclamation since slavery. Long before slaves ever possessed a pulpit, they made use of the enormous stage of life. Every meeting place, ranging from slave quarters to stumps in the woods, became a platform to discuss the impending judgment of God upon their oppressors and the expectant justice of freedom. After emancipation, slaves no longer had to hide in the woods or convene in secrecy, as the first of the Negro churches began to spring up in the south. From its inception, history reveals the Negro church at the center of black life.

The black church was the central station for the black community, the grooming agent for all activism, and the nurturing parent to our political leadership. Our history is reflective of the church as a political incubator, as it was not uncommon then or now for pastors to participate in electoral and non-electoral politics. The ethos of the black church at many levels embraces politics. This is in part due to the fact that from its inception, the black church opposed slavery and racial discrimination that was legalized by public policies and laws. Plainly stated, the black church was innately a living contradiction to oppressive laws, and upon its establishment became political in nature, as it fought the legal system for relief and justice. Historic platform preachers of the Reconstruction Era like Frederick Douglass, Hiram Rhoades Revels, Harriet Tubman, and Sojourner Truth, to contemporary preachers like the Reverends Jesse Jackson and Al Sharpton, all have shared both the pulpit and the platform. The work of the public theologian is to liberate the masses to full citizenship. Like the prophets of old, they hold the responsibility of bringing our nation back to a God-consciousness.

Prophetic Voice

We are able to communicate the love of God from secular spaces because of an enduring commitment to the heirloom responsibility of proclaiming salvation and serving as prophets. A prophet, by all biblical accounts, confronted societal ills as well as chided faltering priests and the indifferent religious community. A prophet "reminds me, that somebody must bring God to man, and say, 'Thus saith the Lord.'"[42] This is the voice of the prophet, more commonly referred to as prophetic voice. While one can suggest that a pulpit preacher is primarily a priest, bringing people back to God and serving as a mediator, the platform preacher has a different mission. The prophetic voice of the platform preacher is one of confrontation. The prophetic voice is the direct vocalization of truth and justice. Truth pronounced to the poor is that justice is a reality, while impeding judgment is proclaimed to the agents of corruption and oppression. The impending judgment may result from the direct actions of resistance to oppression or mass crises, due to indifference. In a real sense, the proclamation of truth and justice is salvific information. Dr. king once stated, "Who is it that is supposed to articulate the longings and aspirations of the people more than the preacher."[43] Platform preachers make known the needs of the people, in order that they might be "saved."

Expensive Taste: Speaking the Truth at All Costs

Additionally, to be effective in the goal of offering salvation, we must consider the prophetic voice as a tool to aid in the elevation and advancement for blacks and all humanity. A prophet should remain free to firmly rebuke both the nation and the church of its failures. In the role of prophet, the preacher is fully aware of the consequences. One must willfully place one's political goods at risks. These goods include finance, because stating the truth can place us on a list of least invited and even sanctioned, thereby limiting the amount of potential earnings. Additionally, we place at risk our access. If one receives grants, funding, or governmental support, we must be prepared to stand alone at the loss of such and continue to voice the truth. Finally, we risk our associational ties by deciding to preserve the integrity of our soul and speak to those things that we have come to believe are dear to the heart of God.[44]

When a preacher serves as a prophet, he will often miss the "most popular" list and may actually be considered an outside agitator and/or troublemaker. Because the spoken truth generally has a way of revealing the hypocrisy of those in power, prophets are directly and indirectly seen as responsible for civil outbreaks and the surge for justice. Time and time again, during the civil rights movement, we heard such declarations from white southerners as, "Our city was fine until those uppity negras come down here and stirred up our good negras." The truth is that the city was not fine and it took the truth being presented for the masses to rise up and demand justice. Frederick Douglass was right, "Power concedes nothing without a demand." Those who benefit the greatest from the subordination of others quite often brand those who promote freedom, as extremists. One can find solace in the fact that truth is validated and supported by biblical examples:

Was not Jesus an extremist in love—"love your enemies, bless them that curse you, do good to them that hate you, and pray for them that despitefully use you and persecute?[45]" Was not Amos an extremist for justice—"Let justice roll down like waters and righteousness like a mighty stream?[46]" Was not Paul an extremist for the gospel of Jesus Christ—"I bear in my body the marks of the Lord Jesus?"[47]

The contemporary platform preacher sides with the rejected prophets, apostles, and Jesus. In each case, all were rejected for their political confrontations, civil disobedience, and for their love for God, regardless of personal consequences. The Old Testament informs our voice, as it provides a "Messianic model, a mission-oriented life with an overwhelming conviction to stand as a deliverer of people."[48] The New Testament provides us with the status- and norm-breaking ministry of Jesus. It was the ministry of Jesus that provided king with his ideals of extreme love, as many of his speeches referred to the parables and His love ethic. One should note that prophets closely follow the itinerary preaching style of Jesus, speaking far more in the community than in the synagogue. Ironically, for society to label those who bear the truth as extremists is in line with all biblical history.

Prophets utilize their voice to challenge the status quo of their time. They address the issues of injustice publicly and dramatically—from Moses' confrontation in Pharaoh's court to Elijah's Mount Carmel showdown with the false priests. In each case, public and dramatic confrontation was the method. By all accounts, the prophet's goal is to confront injustice in a two-fold manner, considering both personal and systemic accountability. Thus, we seek to prescribe, not only a personal diagnosis, but a systemic one as well. Our hope is that individuals will personally be "saved" and that those saved people will work toward the salvific reconstruction of America. It is the labor of black preachers to utilize this form of "Jeremiad," the sermonizing of a political message, to hold America accountable to her founding principles, in the sight of God. The platform preacher must remain able to explain the social climate and the sufferings of blacks, while providing a democratic and legally acceptable means of protest against injustice.

It is my contention that the methodology of confrontation and phraseology in articulation has to unquestionably derive more from the example of biblical prophets than any other source. The Bible reminds us to consider the end goal of prophetic confrontation in the public sphere. The goal is to revolutionize the culture, by making known the sins of the nation, in hope that repentance will occur. Repentance, in public theology, is an ownership of offenses committed against others, the total abandonment of such actions, and restitution on behalf of the victimized. The prophet's mandate is to hold the guilty accountable without becoming cemented in blame, finger-pointing, or bitterness. Rather, the mandate is to become cloaked in a love that "promotes reconciliation, redemption, and the creation of a beloved community."[49] king frames the thought with his words, "Something positive must be done; everyone must share in the guilt as individuals and institutions. The government must certainly share the guilt, individuals must share the guilt, even the church must share the guilt."[50] The concept of guilt-sharing brings the broken community into a contrite spirit, forgiving and considering the neighbor. Now, let us turn our attention and examination from platform ministry and the prophetic voice to arguably one of the greatest public theologians in history.

CHAPTER 8

THE LEGACY OF A kING: A VOICE IN THE POLITICAL WILDERNESS

"And he came into all the country about Jordan, preaching the baptism of repentance for the remission of sins; As it is written in the book of the words of Esaias the prophet, saying, The voice of one crying in the wilderness, Prepare ye the way of the Lord, make his paths straight. Every valley shall be filled, and every mountain and hill shall be brought low; and the crooked shall be made straight, and the rough ways shall be made smooth; And all flesh shall see the salvation of God."
—Luke 3:3-6

Inspiring a King

"Train up a Child in the way that he should go: and when he is old, he will not depart from it."
—Proverbs 22:6

It is important to note at the start of this chapter that Dr. king's life is currently in vogue. In his death, he is an iconic figure, representing the ideals of democracy. His words are frequently quoted in television commercials and literature. His image is displayed wherever the cause of love and justice is paramount. The media, along with the academy, highlight his service in many roles, namely civil rights leader, human rights activist, and organizer. But it is essential to understand what king considered himself to be. Before and above all, king was a preacher. His life was a response to the Gospel of Jesus Christ that led him to declare, "Before I was a civil rights leader, I was a preacher of the Gospel. This was my first and it still remains my greatest commitment. You know all that I do in civil rights I do because I consider it a part of my ministry. I have no other ambitions in life but to achieve excellence in the Christian ministry."[51] I make mention of this fact for two reasons. First and foremost, it is to promote the understanding that the ministry of king, albeit agile and adaptive in geographical terms, was rigidly cemented in the role of a Christian preacher. Second, king emphatically states his primary goal is to preach the Gospel, and though operating in many roles, he chose not to abandon the call to preach or serve his local congregation.

Therefore, it is with the words of king in mind that I propose an analysis that is primarily concerned with his service as a preacher, who faithfully served across larger platforms in life. It is my contention that many, with laudable intention, have labeled king in their study as primarily an activist with political goals of justice and democracy. They fail to understand him as an agile preacher, and they are not able to trace his ideals of justice and love to his theology. An appropriate view of king's theological themes will provide insight into his understanding of salvation, which I argue was his ultimate goal. To fully understand king is to investigate his speeches and writings for Christian undertones. Because king was a preacher, it best serves us to draw special attention to his sermons, speeches, and actions. I am in agreement with theologian James Cone who suggests:

What king really thought about God is not found in the essays or even the Ph.D. dissertation he wrote in graduate school and is not found even in some of his published essays and books about the civil rights movement, but one discovers king's faith primarily in his preached word (chiefly the unpublished sermons) delivered at Dexter Avenue, Ebenezer, and other black churches and in his practiced word during many of his non-violent, direct-action demonstrations, mainly in the south.[52]

Cone's analysis highlights king as fundamentally a man of faith, committed to his God and the Church. king proclaimed salvation to two audiences: the sacred and the secular. king's ministry bridged secular and sacred audiences with nominal separation between them at times. Because faith was at the core of king's proclamation, one should consider the genesis of his belief system.

In Christianity, faith is received through the Word of God, as the Apostle Paul writes, "faith comes by hearing and hearing by the Word of God."[53] Therefore, king's faith did not evolve by happenstance, but rather developed over time from three pertinent influences, the Negro church, black Christian activism, and the Christian social gospel. These major sources continue to influence the agile ministry preachers up to the present age. king's life was indeed influenced, so much that a calling was solidified and a preacher emerged, who proclaimed salvation to the world. Thus, king's agile ministry was a result of his being reared in a family and community where social engagement was a part of the ethos for preachers.

The Development of a King

"And the child grew and became strong, filled with wisdom; and the favor of God was upon him."

—St. Luke 2:40

When one speaks of the reception of "calling," the spiritual heart-felt revelation and understanding that one is to serve God in a particular manner, one has to also examine circumstances and influences that lead one to such an acceptance. In the case of king, his call was to preach the Gospel, and his family was instrumental in providing examples that could be emulated. In reflection of his own call, king suggests, "My call to ministry was not a miraculous or supernatural something. On the contrary, it was an inner urge calling me to serve humanity."[54] This inner urge to serve was nurtured and groomed under the tutelage of his parents and grandparents, and in the safety of his total community. king gives credence to this in stating, "Because of the influence of my mother and father, I guess I always had a deep urge to serve humanity, but I didn't start out with an interest to enter the ministry. I thought I could probably do it better as a lawyer or doctor."[55] In addition to the influence of his mother and father, king, as the son of a Baptist minister, also had many preaching examples. Coincidently, both his great-grandfather and grandfather were also Baptist ministers.

As a child, king heard the story of Jesus and witnessed a social consideration, displayed by his elders. For example, Reverend Williams, King's grandfather, courageously founded Atlanta's branch of the National Association for the Advancement of Colored People (NAACP). Such endeavors courted potential beatings, threats, and other hardships, even death, for blacks during segregation. During segregation, the NAACP was seen as a subversive organization that threatened oppressive individuals and systems with courage and constant agitation for justice. King's father, the Reverend king, Sr., whom he lovingly called "Daddy king," was just as courageous and unapologetic in his activism. Daddy king did not view his Christianity as a private expression, reserved only for weekly stained-glass forums. He proclaimed, "The church must touch every phase of community life."[56]

This was the manner in which king grew to understand the Church and the aforementioned heirloom of Christian responsibility. The Negro church was the premier institution in the black community, offering societal hope, help, and salvation. But the Negro church was not his only influence. king's theological framing of "salvation" that would be preached in sacred and secular spheres, also came through his formal education: Morehouse College, Crozer Theological Seminary, and Boston University School of Theology. It was in seminary that king was exposed to the concept of the Christian social gospel.

In time, king accepted the totality of his call to peach the Gospel and believed with all sincerity that the Christian preacher had a responsibility to address both the spiritual and the social needs of society. The work of saving the soul and body prompted king to say, "The projection of a social gospel is the true witness of a Christian life."[57] In seminary, king embraced the theological underpinning of the Gospel that suggested, "Christianity would no longer be grounded in an ascetic gospel, preaching only an exclusive message of individual salvation. Rather, the Church would pursue the social hope of Jesus and the primitive Church to embrace the world and to transform it with a radical new message of salvation."[58] In time, king developed an appreciation of the early framers of the social gospel believing that the Gospel of Jesus Christ would work to alleviate social, political, and economic problems.[59]

However, king realized the limitations of the social gospel in the realm of praxis and engaged in a new brand of the social gospel, one that king would embody in noteworthy fashion throughout his life. In king's studies, he gained "all the attributes of a social gospeler, a stringent criticism of capitalism, an empathy for the working poor, a love of God, and a commitment to leading people into a life and death struggle for equality and development as full-fledged citizens."[60] However, it should be noted that king "employed some of the theology of the social gospel, while at the same time, rejecting the white supremacy implicit in it."[61]

Later in king's life, he used the term Christian social gospel in his writings and dialogue. He did so with an understanding of all its intricate history. The term served his purposes of gaining the support of white Protestant liberals, who were familiar with the term, to become actively engaged in the freedom movement. Therefore, king arose as someone being "deeply influenced by the social gospel, yet articulated a distinctive brand,"[62] while employing the theology and praxis of black Christian social activists. In conclusion, we recognize that both the Negro church with its black Christian activism and the social gospel contributed greatly to king's proclamation. With this in mind, we move from an analysis of his development to examine his role as a preacher and how he proclaimed salvation across platforms.

CHAPTER 9

RULES OF ENGAGEMENT

"Behold, I send you forth as sheep in the midst of wolves: be ye therefore wise as serpents, and harmless as doves."
                                                    —Matthew 10:16

Rules of Engagement: Keys to Effective Public Theology

There are several norms that will exist in profitable public theology: democratic vision, social analysis, acts of resistance or emancipation, and acts of reconciliation.[63] king revealed a robust democratic vision in his public speeches and sermons, often conveying a deep longing to acquire full citizenship through the principles of democracy. He was able to unite, in seamless motion, the theology founded in the words of the prophets, apostles, and Jesus, with the words of the framers of the Constitution and Declaration of Independence. For example, king's, "I Have a Dream" speech is one of the best documents for explaining the norm of a democratic vision.

He begins his speech by rendering honor to the crafters of American democracy by noting, "When the architects of our republic wrote the magnificent words of the Constitution and the Declaration of Independence, they were signing a promissory note to which every American was to fall heir. This note was the promise that all men, yes black men as well as white men, would be guaranteed the unalienable rights of life, liberty, and the pursuit of happiness."[64] At times, the speech blends both patriotic rhetoric and pastoral principles. An example of this combination is found in the following words: "This will be the day when all God's children will be able to say with new meaning, 'My country 'tis of thee; sweet land of liberty; of thee I sing; land where my fathers died, land of the pilgrims pride; from every mountain side, let freedom ring.' And if America is to be a great nation, this must be true."[65]

It is interesting to note how king's public theology was concerned about saving America, in the sense that she would be saved from the sin and shame of injustice and hatred. In fact, the slogan, "Save the Soul of America" was adopted as the mission and mantra of the Southern Christian Leadership Conference. The importance of the democratic vision in public theology evolves from the notion that certain biblical principles of justice are shared in democratic ideals. It is in the sharing of ideals that "religious warrants can be introduced into public argument in a way compatible with the fundamental values of democracy, congenial to the diversity of political and moral positions, and comfortable to basic standards of publicity."[66]

In addition to the democratic vision, public theology provides a social analysis. Because king was a member of the society of the oppressed, his articulation of the lived experience is especially noteworthy. In king's "Letter from the Birmingham Jail," he crafted a compelling argument in response to a group of white clergy, who urged king to slow down the movement. He summed up his reasons for not doing so with powerful examples of the endured disrespect and degradation of blacks. He states, "When you are hurried by day and haunted by night by the fact that you are a Negro...when you are forever fighting a degenerating sense of 'nobodiness,' then you will understand why we find it difficult to wait."[67] king's social analysis is not limited to color or creed, but encompassed various segments of society. He possessed the courage to speak the truth, even to the Church.

In his *Eulogy for the Martyred Children*," of the Sixteenth Street Baptist Church," king began by criticizing the clergy who had remained silent. He further indicted the racist and hate-filled politicians and hypocritical government. Finally, he ended with a critical charge of inaction toward Negroes, who were not involved in the struggle for civil rights. Although poetically rendered, he painted the dreadful social setting wherein this atrocity occurred. The social analysis is an acknowledgment of power and powerlessness. The analysis is what the public theologian uses to confront agents of injustice. Without a stark and real depiction of the state-of-being in society, both the sacred and the secular will be reluctant to engage in action.

The next category of public theology is the move toward acts of resistance or emancipation. An examination of king's work reveals two primary methods that he utilized in resistance: the prophetic voice and non-violent direct action. The prophetic voice for king was the mandate to transmit the desires of God and a process of revealing the sins of the nation. The revelation of sin promotes repentance, a complete abandonment of oppressive and exploitative actions both personally and through public policy. In the kingian lens, true repentance occurs when ownership of offenses occurs.

The prophetic voice is not concerned with placing blame, but in transforming society. Holding the nation accountable enables people to choose the rightness of justice by responding with affirming actions. The alternative is the acceptance of the injustice that inevitably brings about the judgment of God. Admittedly, the phrase, "the judgment of God," is highly theological and is usually reserved for sacred settings. Yet, in public theology, it can be best described as the realized consequences of indifference to mass violence, poverty, sickness, despair, and oppression. Black preachers, since their beginning in America, have believed in a living God, who will judge the oppressor on behalf of the oppressed. This form of preaching is prophetic in essence and political in realization. king utilized this form of preaching or "Jeremiad" more effectively than any other proponent in the twentieth century. I say this, fully aware that king stood on the shoulders of his fore bearers to reach that level of mass recognition and communication. What one finds in king is an ability to explain both the climate and the suffering of blacks, while at the same time, provide a legal means of public protest against the African-American predicament. The modes and methods of emancipation expressed by king were developed in extreme times and warranted extreme measures to fulfill the work of justice.

I submit a warning here and note, as a public theologian, that if one stands as an advocate, he or she must, not only acknowledge the cries of the people, but must ultimately respond to the voice of God. Beware. The waters of public theology can become murky in that clergy may confuse the voice of the people with the ultimate voice of God. Make no mistake: There is a difference between the voice of God and the voice of the people. The public theologian must discern who is speaking, because the Christian must always yield ultimate allegiance to God. king, hearing the aspirations of the people, responded with "God speech," being both dutiful in regard to humanity, and offering a devout love for God. He endured sharp criticisms for engaging in service that others deemed unchristian and beyond the bounds of a preacher. He found solace by stating, "Ultimately, a genuine leader is not a searcher of consensus, but a molder of consensus...There comes a time when one must take the position that is neither safe, nor politic, nor popular, but he must do it because conscience tells him it is right."[68] king brings to light the reality of serving in the public sphere. It is one of hearing the longings of the people, but responding to the voice of God.

Finally, king's public theology also included acts of reconciliation. It becomes obvious as one examines the life of king, that he was not interested in retribution, but in redemption. What makes his articulation of redemption acceptable is that he does not render the commandment to "love your enemies," while standing outside the struggle. He speaks as one who has been through the "fire," or in theological terms, born his "cross" in a Christ like manner. He sought to foster reconciliation and usher in the "Beloved Community," the realized state of existence where all members of society share justice and peace. king's belief in the biblical concept that "unearned suffering is redemptive" proved to promote his public theology and win over opponents, as others found better understanding of God through his suffering for the oppressed. On one occasion, he outlined his suffering in Pauline fashion, "I've been in more than eighteen jail cells. Since that time, I've come perilously close to death at the hands of a demented Negro woman. Since that time, I've seen my home bombed three times. Since that time, I've had to live everyday under the threat of death. Since that time, I've had many frustrating and bewildering nights."[69] This laundry list of suffering highlights the fact that his love was forged in immense pain and heartache. king, as a platform minister, was able to speak the language of democracy and citizenship from a heartfelt conviction of biblically-inspired justice. This was his gift to us—a model of public theology that helps to change unjust public policy, to lift the low, and make plain the paths needed by the wounded masses in their walk to freedom. Yes, public theology is needed in today's societal discourse, not just because king utilized it or even that it has a unique history, but more than anything, because it is necessary. Our voices must be heard beyond the pulpit if we are to realize the expectation of our prayers and lead our nation out of the political wilderness.

This being the case, platform oration for the black preacher is a montage of both public and private interests. Thus, the black church and the preacher have a vested interest in the word "public," as it pertains to the associational life and seeks to address issues of the polis broadly conceived and to engage the broad interests and concerns of citizens.[70] Therefore, historically, there was little option for separation of Church and state, as it pertains to the Negro church, since the church had the only accessible space to meet the public needs of Negroes. Because the rule of the day was segregation, the Negro church, by law not choice, became a one-stop shop. It was the central location for mental edification, social direction, financial stabilization, and spiritual enlightenment.

The Negro preachers of old were in their bones naturally political. Their DNA has intrinsically been transferred to black gospel preachers of succeeding generations. Contemporary public theologians like Rev. Dr. Gardner C. Taylor, Rev. Dr. Charles G. Adams, former Congressman Rev. Floyd Flake, and State Senator James Meeks, all have been directly involved in electoral politics. Their churches are significant communal institutions, because they have what oppressive systems fear: informed, engaged, and organized parishioners with social capital. The rich legacy of our fore bearers is the treasure of concurrent public and private interests.

When one witnesses the work of public theologians, one discovers a relevant gospel of community building. The Church has the potential of being a political force, whether or not the pastor participates in electoral politics. This was true of king, who through his work in the Montgomery Improvement Association and the Southern Christian Leadership Conference, was able to influence policy that effected the successful desegregation of public transportation in Montgomery, Alabama, and created an influential movement that led to the 1963 Civil Rights Act and the 1964 Voting Rights Act. The advantage of church involvement in the building of viable communities uniquely aligns the eternal salvation of one's soul with the natural salvation of one's body. It is a proclamation that works to rescue people from a "hell on earth" experience of life. The platform enables the preacher and the church to serve the larger community, thereby enriching our daily life. The structure of king's public presentations strategically injects biblical text into current social issues, bringing relevance to the text, directive critique of oppression, and hope to the situation. Platform preachers are, in fact, universal communicators.

The platform preacher promotes a spiritual and physical salvation through love-centered action. Theologically, the following scripture provides a foundation from which to define expressive deeds: "And they, continuing daily with one accord in the temple, and breaking bread from house to house, did eat their meat with gladness and singleness of heart. Praising God, and having favor with all the people. And the Lord added to the church daily such as should be saved."[71] The church in the New Testament book of the Acts of the Apostles was a cornerstone for service. Acts chapter 2 outlines the empowerment of the Holy Spirit for worship and work. The work consists both of relief and empowerment for the community. Likewise, contemporary churches should offer such non-discriminatory services to the public, as affordable housing, education enhancing programs, healthcare screenings, employment readiness, and advocacy for children and the elderly.

At this point, it is important to revisit the term "platform theology." As stated earlier, I have taken the core of what is now known as public theology, which is "the engagement of a living religious tradition with its public environment—the economic, political, and cultural spheres of our common life,"[72] and extended that definition to incorporate the directive discourse of the pulpit. This extension arises from the need to ensure that the connection of the platform and the church is not discarded. Thus, the platform theologian is an extension of the pulpit into secular spaces, making available holistic salvation for all. It is important to note that we develop our platform theology under the tutelage of the pulpit, being able to communicate the love of God through active community-building without drawing distinctive lines to separate the secular or the sectarian.

Finally, the community-building efforts of the public theologian demands that preachers stand with the least economically stable in the community. It should be noted that king's assassination occurred, as he stood in solidarity with black sanitation workers in Memphis, TN, as he led "The Poor Peoples Campaign." The leader, who championed integration, desegregation, and voting rights, exerted enormous pressure on policy makers, to secure economic justice for the masses, known as the working poor. king encouraged empowerment through gainful employment and livable wages. It was his persistence in this area, along with the ability to mobilize the masses into direct action, that ultimately led to his assassination on that infamous day in Memphis. His was a call for complete freedom—a severing of the umbilical cord of dependence, more often used to strangle the life and money out of people, rather than supply nourishment. His call was an effort to cast off the heavy burden of bearing the nation's wealthy on the backs of the laboring poor. In like manner, today's preacher must seek to empower individuals and build vibrant self-sufficient communities. We should be willing to use resources from various sources, refusing to be dependent upon anyone. Our platform ministry must exercise the intrinsic power of the black church and the community, in that we utilize the fundamental, but often latent, resources of people, money, and organization. This is the work of the community builder, and it is from this platform that God's kingdom is realized without discrimination of creed, color, status, or religious beliefs for all people.

PAVEMENT

CHAPTER 10

WORD ON THE STREET

"And the lord said unto the servant, Go out into the highways and the hedges, and compel them to come in, that my house may be filled."

—Luke 14:23

There Goes the Neighborhood!

"And, behold, a certain lawyer stood up, and tempted him, saying, Master, what shall I do to inherit eternal life? He said unto him, What is written in the law? how readest thou? And he answering said, Thou shalt love the Lord thy God with all thy heart, and with all thy soul, and with all thy strength, and with all thy mind; and thy neighbour as thyself. And he said unto him, Thou hast answered right: this do, and thou shalt live. But he, willing to justify himself, said unto Jesus, And who is my neighbour?"

—St. Luke 10:25-29

The Faith-Based Coalition of the University Area Community Center in Tampa, Florida sits as an oasis in the middle of what has become known as "Suit Case City." The negative phrase is commonly used by surrounding local residents and serves as a moniker for the highly-transient neighborhood. It is the typical story of most urban centers in the United States. The community has undergone several population changes in terms of ethnicity. The economics of the community are greatly limited by the lack of a stable tax base, provided by businesses and homeowners. Undocumented residents make up a large percentage of the underground workforce, providing domestic service, landscaping, and any other service that is profitable, but allocated under the table for less than minimum wage. Crime is frequent. For instance, on Friday nights, men and women carry on their persons the week's pay, making themselves easy prey for muggers. Alcohol is easily accessible from the litter of liquor stores, strategically planted to keep the ailing intoxicated. Pawnshops, rent to owns, payday loans, and check-cashing franchises soak up the very life from the soul and pocketbooks of the residents.

Our work has been simple, offering non-discriminatory services and providing basic needs: clothing, food, medical attention, and housing—all critical to maintaining a sense of humanity. Additionally, we have been able to offer education, job training, and cultural awareness to parents and their children. Our goal is the restoration of the broken community and the reality of neighborhood. There is some difficulty in reattaching the word, "neighbor," to what we so frequently refer to as the "hood." Everyday, we are working collectively with other institutions to dig a well of stability where all members of the community can draw buckets of self-respect, consideration, hope, family, and love unrestricted. There is no other means to restore a sense of community than to base it upon "neighbor."

And Who Is My Neighbor?

The premier principle embedded in the scripture text of the Gospel of St. Luke (10:25-29) evolves from the manner in which Jesus used the word, "neighbor." Jesus clarifies the definition of the word by revealing what community and a godly life should reflect in daily living. An inquisitive scribe facetiously attempts to draw Jesus into a discussion of "eternal life," in an effort to prove his selfish philosophy of selectivity. However, Jesus advises the scribe to answer his own question "according to the Law." The answer to the scribe's question speaks to a totality of commitment to love God with one's heart, soul, strength, mind, and possess a nondiscriminatory love of neighbor as oneself. Again, Jesus affirms that loving God requires one to love all people indiscriminately, unconditionally, and universally. All humanity then becomes his neighbor. Jesus emphatically defines love as, not simply a noun, but also a verb—an ethic of action and movement solely for the good of others.

The Church has the responsibility of reminding its members that their neighbors are not just the ones who sit next to them for two hours on Sunday morning, neither are they limited to the polite man nor woman who waves, as you pull into your suburban gated community. When Christ speaks of neighbors, there is a sense of the Asiatic history and cultural norms of rendering hospitable service and assistance to all those you encounter. We must keep in mind that we are all sojourners, and it is only a matter of time when life presents a set of circumstances that requires a hand from those who cross our paths. A selective view of one's neighbor is the result of socio-philosophical fence-building that excludes most and hides the true quality of humanity from our spiritual view. Our jobs, positions, neighborhoods, churches, and so-called success can blind our perception. More often than not, the poor, broken, and homeless are viewed as failing to capitalize on the grand opportunity of living in America. In short, we can subconsciously ascribe to the view that they deserve their unfortunate lot, while we seek to help only those who appear to be lifting themselves up by their bootstraps, to escape the pit of despair. The so-called bootstrap philosophy is only as strong as the sociological bootstraps. The philosophy falls utterly short and serves no real value, when people are literally stripped and stand naked before a world of opportunity with no bootstraps to grasp.

Help, We've Fallen and Can't Get Up!

"And Jesus answering said, A certain man went down from Jerusalem to Jericho, and fell among thieves, which stripped him of his raiment, and wounded him, and departed, leaving him half dead."
—Luke 10:30

Jesus, in light of the question presented by the scribe, begins to teach the principle of love through the telling of a parable. In such, Jesus reveals that a man has been the unfortunate victim of crime. He is robbed, wounded, and left for dead on the Jericho road. Interestingly, the text declares that this man "fell" among thieves. The victim did not plan the unfortunate circumstance, there was no time to prepare, and like the swift transition of the wind on a gusty March morning, a drastic occurrence was thrust upon him as he journeyed. I dare say this is the reality for most people who exist on the fringes of life. They "fall" among thieves. It is unimaginable to suggest that a person contemplates, develops strategizes, plans, and executes his or her personal, economic, familial, educational, and spiritual demise. Surely, one can argue that some are in tragic denial and often stand in rebellion against the very people or institutions that are genuinely concerned about their personhood. However, the rebellion of the dejected is a reaction most commonly rendered out of immature, nonsensical thinking in response to a hostile world or occurs when a person believes that his or her support networks have diminished. In light of the reality of rebellion, the truth remains that most people who are down, not only need help, but actually want help as well.

When all support and protection are removed, people essentially "fall" among thieves. This particular text reveals the downward spiral of a neighborhood gone awry. However, the text moves from tragic victimization to possibility and redemption. Jesus sets the scene, and its outcome is determined by the efforts and concerns of those, who journeyed along this treacherous stretch of highway from Jerusalem to Jericho. Here lies a man, who has just been robbed of his possessions and denied the freedom granted to him by his legal right to economic surety. He is stripped of his divine right of human dignity. He is wounded, due to a lack of protection from the violence of others. He lays motionless. His moans of pain are few and far between. His near lifeless body is a silhouette, barely distinguishable from the outlines of the desert shrubbery. He can neither help himself nor can he pull himself up, despite the proverbial moralistic taunting of the so-called well-to-doers. If this man is to live, regain that which was lost, and become self- sufficient again, someone has to intervene. For this man, it was the Samaritan. For the waylaid in today's society, it is the grand opportunity for the Church.

Religious Reluctance

"And by chance there came down a certain priest that way; and when he saw him, he passed by on the other side. And likewise a Levite, when he was at the place, came and looked on him, and passed by on the other side."

— Luke 10:31

On that dark and dusty road, a tragedy occurred. This vicious attack ironically provided an opportunity for someone to administer care and concern for the wounded. By chance, two persons—one a priest and the other a Levite—both ordained for service to God and the people, have been presented a divine opportunity. Although the first to arrive on the scene, they passed by and witnessed firsthand the dire need of the wounded. However, they ultimately decided that the social or religious risk of assisting the man in need was too great. Many theologians and scholars have argued that the priest and Levite feared the man was dead, and by touching the deceased, they would break covenantal Levitical laws, thus disqualifying them for future service to God and His people. The argument is indeed logical, however, the parable does not reveal that the men displayed any concern or made any attempt to determine whether or not the man was in fact dead. Actually, the text uses the phrase, "passed by on the other side," after they saw the wounded man. The original language of the text indicates that they crossed the road intentionally, to avoid the problem, averting their eyes from that which had already been witnessed by their souls. Indeed, they purposely crossed to the other side of the road. How often has the Church responded in similar fashion?

How often have we looked upon people and refused to see them? Yes, see them in all of their being: in anguish, failure, and hope for survival. Does the Church possess the ability to see potential in the most victimized of the community? Does the Church have the divine gift to look beneath the surface and see more than the ragged clothing, disgruntled actions, and disturbing realities of self-hatred? And upon seeing such, can we tap into the endless possibilities that lie within all who have fallen? The act of bringing redemption to the lost and hope to the hopeless cannot be accomplished from afar. There has to be face-to-face, heart-to-heart encounters, where one is close enough to see an opportunity to do something good, as well as acknowledge the wounded as candidates for recovery, redemption, and reconciliation. If they cannot be seen as worthy of personal risk, then society will forever live with the debilitating disease of selective blindness.

Moved by Compassion

"But a certain Samaritan, as he journeyed, came where he was: and when he saw him, he had compassion on him, And went to him, and bound up his wounds, pouring in oil and wine, and set him on his own beast, and brought him to an inn, and took care of him."

—*St. Luke 10:33-34*

Jesus does not hide or overlook the blatant blindness of the religious order. Rather, He chooses in this parable to introduce an agent, who was not an ordained cleric. He was an unlikely hero, a Samaritan, of all people—a man from an ethnicity of people who were both rejected and despised by Jews. Yet, the Samaritan chose to see what others had refused to notice: that some cases of assault might leave one down, but not out.

The Church must see beyond the surface. Its gaze into the lives of people should be with such compassion that one cannot help but to be moved from within. When the Gospel writer uses the word, "compassion," it means to be moved from within, to be drawn into action on behalf of another, without debate, dialogue, or discussion. It is demonstrative of the kind of associative love that, having previously weighed the cost of responding to others, now becomes a spontaneous reaction to the present need. This kind of "compassion" translates into a neighborly love that speaks extemporaneously in action, needing neither a confirmation nor an affirmation of outside sources before administering grace.

Thus, the Samaritan draws closer, bridges the gap, and closes the distance between himself and the wounded man, seeing their circumstances easily interchangeable. No wonder our fore bearers taught us to say, "There but for the grace of God, go I!" The final scene of the parable reveals that the Samaritan accepted the risk of vulnerability, ambush, and assault, to dutifully administer aide on that dangerous and dusty roadside. The one who is dismissed as being subhuman is often the one who restores the dignity of humanity to others. The parable of the "Good Samaritan" is an extraordinary example of thinking "outside the box," where the ministry of Jesus utilizes non- traditional exemplars to challenge the religious status quo of His day. His was a mobile ministry of intentional location, presence, solidarity, and intervention, which is the rudimentary core of all pavement theology.

But how does one put into operation the example of pavement theology exposed by Jesus in the parable of the Good Samaritan? Although we have entered into the twenty-first century, the concepts of intentional location, presence, solidarity, and intervention are just as vital and needed as when the parable was first spoken. Many have expressed, in one form or another, this typology of ministry. In the twentieth century, king embodied the best of the lasting legacy of intentional location. His work was found in movement, touching the lives of the masses outside the church walls. His was a mission to make salvation available to countless individuals, who would probably never step foot into a sanctuary. Since his untimely departure, we seek to capture and resurrect the essence of "dwelling among the people" for redemption's sake.

Intentional Location

Throughout the liberation movement, men and women have intentionally placed themselves in the midst of hostile and inhumane conditions. Sages like Harriet Tubman, who, upon her escape from slavery, returned time and time again, entering into hell's gate to set the captives free. She exhibited the audacity to defy all sensibilities and place at risk the very thing that one would risk death to gain. For the freedom movement, Harriet Tubman's life's lesson to us is that, as long as injustice exists, all freedom is at risk. king understood this and practiced intentional location in southern bastions of bigotry: Birmingham, Montgomery, Albany, and throughout Mississippi. His actions helped to define love as a principle of purposefully positioning oneself to physically engage societal norms of injustice. The work to establish a just civil order, capable of providing relief for damages and loss from crimes against the souls and bodies of people, requires a life of divine assignment. The embedded agent has but one assignment: Provide avenues for the immediate rescue of the afflicted and the reconciliation of the broken community.

The mission of king was evidenced by his choices to live and work among the poor, who dwell in the cold and dark basement of the world's house. There, the isolated only catch porthole glimpses of a locked stairway, guarded by the rule of the rich that, if accessed, could elevate them to a better tomorrow. The citizenry of the oppressed exist throughout the world. king, realizing this, traveled extensively, preaching the good news to the rejected, outcasts, and the downtrodden. His life became one of airports, automobiles, and the protest march—his most noted mode of transformation when covering both political and physical ground.

The protest march enhanced king's understanding of community and provided him with the concept of the shared experience, more than any other religious or intellectual institution he attended. The unified foot-stepping, singing, and praying enabled king to form a cohesive bond with the hurting and exploited masses. In the sphere of the pavement, king became a witness to faith, hope, and love, as well as the opposing evil of hatred and bigotry. It should be noted that this "walking out of ministry" does not necessarily have to take place on physical pavement, but it does require one to be present with people in suffering. It requires a willingness to be intentionally located in the struggle for human dignity. This is the call of the pavement preacher, and it is one that king fully embraced. In each step, the Gospel was preached, as the message of the Lord became tangible and touchable in the flesh of committed servants. The legacy of the protest march resides in the fact that action was taken with the human body and not simply in words. It was a movement fueled by figuratively walking from the straw pits of Egypt, the drudgery of second-class citizenship, into the Promised Land: a destination where Pharaoh's dominance of racism, monarchy of wealth, and despotic control would rein no more. king's work and walk helped to lead the masses into the milk and honey of full citizenship.

A Conscious Decision

As king completed the required course work at Boston University, he began to weigh the options of whether to enter the pastorate in the north or the south. He pondered the benefit of receiving an education in the north and finding a parish ministry to serve out his calling. The north would provide an atmosphere where the brutal arm of Jim Crow south would be a painful, but distant reality. Besides, one could possibly earn a better salary and take advantage of additional socio-economic opportunities, particularly with his attained education. On the other hand, in the south, lay king's hope for change and his connection to a rich history of the Negro in America. Ultimately, king and his wife Coretta decided to return south. This would be king's first step toward becoming a pavement minister.

His decision was to intentionally locate himself through conscious and deliberate choice, preferably in a place with suffering people. king understood that for a black man to return to the south meant that he would immediately place his life in the cradle of black suffering and put his neck of opportunity into the systemic lynch noose of hatred. king's decision to locate in the south was based on an eschatological hope. His longing would join his fore bearer's expectation of liberation. The hope would continue to swell in the belly of the universe, creating a chain reaction that would become manifest in mass organization and conscious acts of liberation.

Thus, "he returned to the deep south, not entirely happy about moving to Montgomery, a city still steeped in white supremacy and with few pretensions of new south modernity."[73] It is important to note that the intention of pavement ministry does not require one to be blissful in the location. Actually, one can argue that the opposite seems to be more the norm. However, those who choose to locate in suffering or reject detachment, because of their upward mobility, strive for the optimum possibility in life, which is to share salvation with others. In fact, they valiantly carry out the mission of Jesus, as His earthly location provided salvific hope and human consideration, as He engaged the *least of these.*

However, one must possess a willingness to share a common experience with the disadvantaged and dispossessed. Obviously, king's middle-class background and education provided him a more advantageous future and additional options than that of the average Negro in the south. Nevertheless, it was in the setting of the segregated south that the Negro Ph.D. and the "no D" rubbed shoulders, laughed, cried, mourned, and lived. No gained or inherited attribute unified their existence more than the color of their skin. king willfully joined the masses in Montgomery in suffering the discrimination of the day.

Throughout his life, king made additional moves of intentional location. Once, during the bus boycott, Daddy king,[74] fearing for his son's life after learning that a decision had been made by king's colleagues to voluntarily submit to incarceration by the police, summoned a cadre of Martin's influential mentors and friends to deter him from returning to Montgomery. To intentionally locate with suffering people takes a considerable amount of courage and commitment, in the face of fear, to confront extreme danger. To wit is king's statement, "I must go back to Montgomery. My friends and associates are being arrested. It would be the height of cowardice for me to stay away. I would rather be in jail ten years than desert my people now. I have begun the struggle, and I can't turn back. I have reached the point of no return."[75] Courage was found, not by simply returning to a violent city, but in the understanding that confrontation with violence would be enacted in the mode of non-violent direct action. Thus, his participation in the struggle to relieve the suffering of the poor sacrificially placed his life in harm's way.

Courage and commitment to intentionally locate demand a reason for living beyond oneself. The confrontation between oppressed people and the oppressor invokes extreme sacrifice and superimposes risk above personal safety. It takes conscientious thought and full understanding for one to decide to contribute to the deliverance of others. Our independent choices never exist alone. Rather, they are gracefully formed by time and circumstance, until they are forged into necessary commitment to the cause and livelihood of others. king described this calling when he stated, "If a man doesn't have something that he'll die for, he isn't fit to live."[76] king understood that the "cause," the existence of a just and love-centered society, will always involve freedom for the individual and the total well-being of all people. At no time should the two counteract each other or become separated. The "cause of justice and love" is considered noble, because these actions are made relevant and real only when actualized in the lives of people. Anything less reduces the calling to sentimental gibberish and diminishes the human spirit to a mere sputter of existence that lingers until physical death, which sadly becomes a distorted form of liberation.

In January of 1966, in an effort to keep the cause and consideration of individuals together, king made an intentional decision to locate his family to a slum apartment on the south side of Chicago. In this slum, king's voice rang with authenticity, as he boldly declared, "The purpose of the slum is to confine those who have no power and perpetuate their powerlessness. The slum is little more than a domestic colony that leaves its inhabitants dominated politically, exploited economically, segregated, and humiliated at every turn."[77] The move to Chicago alone speaks of king's commitment to be one with the people, to do what the Old Testament prophet Ezekiel spoke of as, "sitting where they sat."[78] Although king's education and economic background could have been considered hindrances in connecting with the poor, he was able to make the connection by being authentic in his relationships. At no time did he abandon his education and training. His speeches and sermons were replete with Negro culture and history, Western philosophy, and often deep theological queries. His dress, though conservative, revealed a certain class. Yet, in light of this, he maintained the ability to relate to all he encountered. This is the beauty of intentional location; it can birth a ministry of redemptive relationship.

What tends to be overlooked in the protests and the intentional locating of king is this true sense of empathy. Intentional location extends beyond the coming together of mere bodies; it unites spirits and minds with one accord. As a result, Student Nonviolent Coordinating Committee members in sit-ins, the freedom rides, and in the Mississippi Freedom Summer Project devoutly decided to travel into intense persecution. Only sublime empathy would make a person seek opportunities to participate in suffering, knowing the reality of police dogs, clubs, rocks, slurs, dark jail cells, and possible death of such participants. Many stood alongside individuals with whom they had no personal connection, having little in common besides suffering. The pavement preacher, who practices intentional location, does so from the basis of collective responsibility and human consideration. The pavement preacher learns the power of intentionality through shared experience. It is on the pavement that intentional positioning sets the foundation for a ministry that lifts the low, embraces the rejected, and renders the cause of justice and love common to all.

Miracles in Movement

I was introduced to the work that addressed the issue of sin and offered salvation through service in Boston through my trusted friend, the Reverend Mark Jennings. He was a seminarian in residency at the Azusa Christian Community, pastored by Reverend Eugene F. Rivers III. Immediately, Mark thrust himself in the work and history of the movement that Reverends Eugene Rivers, Jeffery Brown, Ray Hammond, and other pastors launched, to stem youth homicide when the streets of Boston were being flooded with the blood of black and brown youth. Their efforts resulted in what is now called the "Boston Miracle," a phrase that was coined to represent the collaborative efforts led by churches in partnership with social service agencies, non-profits, policy makers, and law enforcement. The result was a twenty-nine-month time-span that ended in early January 1998, where no teenage homicides were committed in Boston. The work of the Boston preachers and churches offers insight into a workable model that can be utilized by cities across America.

You Have to Be There!

The agents of the Boston Miracle discovered the ministry of presence. The story goes that, as Rev. Rivers, a fleeing intellectual from Harvard, pitched his tent in the Dorchester neighborhood, he sought out what he calls "a sassy, smart a**, gun slinging mother shut your mouth" by the name of Selvin Brown. What Rivers found in Brown was a "ghetto passport" to introduce him to the neighborhood and one who possessed the street credibility to grant him access into the underground economy of the drug subculture. Ironically, Brown gave the Pentecostal preacher a cynical lesson in why the Church, Christians, clergy, and in his perception, even Christ, were losing the war for the souls and bodies of inner-city youth. The lesson was simple, as Selvin plainly stated to Rivers, "I'm there when Johnny goes out for a loaf of bread for Mama. I'm there, you're not. I win, you lose. It's all about being there."[79] Thus, a ministry of presence was birthed for what would be later called the Ten-point Coalition, as its leadership and a number of other black pastors in the neighborhood mounted a response to the lack of visibility and presence. The preachers began to walk the streets and developed an ear and eye for intervention, as they became a bridge between the police and the community. It is this ministry of presence that makes intervention and salvation possible.

The idea of pastors spending time on the street is not a new phenomenon, as street preachers came to significant recognition during the 1930s through the early 1950s in places like Harlem and Chicago. However, they placed more emphasis on theological and ideological frameworks than practical agency. The ministry of pavement preachers exploded in the mid-fifties and sixties as members of the Student Nonviolent Coordinating Committee, Southern Christian Leadership Conference, and everyday heroes preached sermons one step at a time. The development of pavement preaching continued in flux, as the day of marching protesters dwindled and a new era of street preachers sought to station themselves, not just for a dramatic march, but also for daily ministry. The pavement preacher operates from a community base, but the ministry remains agile and responds with flexibly, in an effort to meet the needs of the most vulnerable. In short, it does not conform to the nine-to-five or Monday through Friday vocational pattern. The ministry of pavement embraces a different work schedule. One must be able to be with the people during the struggle. Such was the strength of Fannie Lou Hamer, the Vice Chairman of the Mississippi Freedom Democratic Party (MFDC), a woman of pure virtue, who possessed a relentless commitment to stay connected to suffering and the advancement of the people, declaring,

"...only a person living in the state of Mississippi knows what it is like to suffer; knows what it is like to be hungry; knows what it is like to have no clothing to wear. And these people in Mississippi State, they are not "down"; all they need is a chance. And I am determined to give my part, not for what the movement can do for me, but what I can do for the movement to bring about a change in the State of Mississippi."[80]

She spoke from the depths of personal experience, authenticating the reality of the savagery inflicted upon a people. When she declared that she was "sick and tired of being sick and tired," she did so by deploring the pain of the poor. Hamer verifies that one dare not speak "on behalf of," unless one is willing to accept "being" one of the scorned, a fact unrealized by many liberal whites of the sixties. Indeed, one cannot voice from a distance. One has to come into close contact with the problem, in order to be heard. One cannot conclude, however, that being present is enough; intervention must take place if salvation is to become a reality.

Divine Intervention through Human Interaction

The work of Rev. Rivers and the cadre of clergy men and women is significant because another wave of street-walking preachers are being developed to combat the forces that drain the hope of young black and brown youth in the street. The current statistics of youth violence in Philadelphia, Baltimore, Chicago, Boston, and southern metropolitan cities demand involvement and action, to reach the perpetrators and victims. The youth of this present age have no involvement with or concern regarding our churches, choirs, or religious rhetoric. They have little or no patience for preachers in general. In their eyes, the preacher is a ghost, someone who is spoken about and rarely seen, except for the all too frequent funeral service. In an effort to offset this tragic dilemma, the pavement offers the preacher an opportunity to be an informed agent of transformation. It provides the preacher with a process that enables one to move from simply speaking about gang members, thugs, drug addicts, the homeless, and the hurting, to actually speaking with them. The model that Jesus presented is one that, not only spoke to the undesirables, but also dined, fellowshipped, and restored them through intimate and frequent interaction. The world cannot afford aloof pristine preachers, who live fearfully in seclusion. Preachers must venture out of their comfort zones and touch a world in dire need.

In the summer of 2004, in the Boston community of Dorchester, Rev. Mark Jennings called a few of his friends together for a meeting. All in attendance were young preachers, eager to make real our witness. We assembled in a former crack house, now Azusa Christian Community Church, and committed ourselves to being one with the people. Every Friday night, we gathered at 9:00 p.m. to begin our service. We targeted areas where the violence and disturbance were most frequent. We wore black suits and white clergy collars, so that we would not be confused with a gang, especially at night, when a group of young men walking may readily be seen as an intrusion into restricted territory. The group walked in and out of communities, stopping briefly and praying under streetlights. We walked until midnight. The first few Fridays, people just stared and paid us little or no attention, except to discern whether or not we were undercover agents, operating some type of sting. As we walked, we offered few words, generally just to, "keep your head up out here. Be safe and make it home tonight." In time, the people began to look forward to seeing us. They began speaking to us and saying how glad they were to see clergy on the street. Young men began to ask for help for youth programming, jobs, and advocacy work in police-to-community relations. Since the goal of our group was to make the connection, not to build our separate memberships, we decided to let the residents approach us for prayer or discussions about church. Sure enough, they began to ask for prayer and assistance. That summer, we witnessed the impact of "churches on the street," a term that Mark coined that has garnered lasting memories for the band of young clergy.

So many young preachers in our churches could use an opportunity to learn and minister to the public. Rather than fighting over the few microphone opportunities in worship or arguing over who is going to read the scripture or pray, let us use our creative energies on the street. The work does not require a budget or degreed leadership, just a willingness to be with people. I suggest that the training ground for the pulpit should include a prerequisite of pavement service. It is best to have some experimental training, and a very real understanding that the streets are no place for religious Rambos or heroes. A pavement preacher, while on the street, will witness illegal drug use and sales, or come face-to-face with gangs and persons under the influence of narcotics. In such cases, one should let wisdom, respect, and spiritual gifts govern interaction, as we seek to see the person behind these actions. Remember, an overall prayerful and considerate demeanor needs to prevail in most cases.

The secular training for pavement ministry should involve an eclectic gathering of methods from strategists, rather than being taken solely from one program or original thinker. The best work on the street is often a result of combing through volumes of abolitionist rescue missions and post-emancipation liberation theory. Furthermore, techniques of endurance and solidarity should be excavated from the slave insurrections, Marcus Garvey's back to Africa movement, the Nation of Islam's self-sufficiency, Malcolm X's "By any means necessary" value system, Martin Luther king's non-violent direct action, and the Black Panther Party's neighborhood policing, children's breakfast, and education programs. Additionally, the pavement preacher would do well to acquire an insatiable appetite for world knowledge from the work of intellectuals, such as W.E.B. Dubois and the social uplift endeavors of Mary McLeod Bethune. But let it be known that no movement among the masses can make a lasting transformation without solidarity, where the many become one.

Solidarity: That We Might Be One

What one finds in Fannie Lou Hamer, Martin Luther king, Jr., and Malcolm X can be described as a sense of authentic agency—the quality of movement that is best expressed in terms of its connected consciousness and pedagogy of the poor. The agent of the Gospel is one that has the propensity to move with the urgency and determination of soul that is not swayed by fear or threat. The quality of all life is bound in each moment, each event, every action for justice, and every grasp toward righteousness. It is the kind of unswerving demeanor that Christ displayed, as He ventured seemingly off course to locate himself at Jacob's Well, by emphatically telling His disciples, "I must needs to go through Samaria."[81] There comes a time in every pavement preacher's life, where actions will even defy logic and reasoning. This kind of movement requires a depth of understanding that is a connected consciousness to those in need.

The entire concept of consciousness hinges on a person's understanding of life. When I speak of life, I am neither speaking of the chronological secession of our days, nor our optimistic ambitions of the American dream of a house, a two-car garage, a white picket fence, and a couple of children. No, when I refer to life, I am specifically speaking about what occurred in the creation narrative of the book of Genesis: "And the Lord God formed man of the dust of the ground, and breathed into his nostrils the breath of life; and man became a living soul."[82] Life is essentially the connection of divinity and humanity, for it was not until the dust was met with the breath of God that man became a living soul. When we are truly alive, we are acutely aware of the God-deposit and painfully cognizant of our humanity and the ever-present potential of being prone to sin. Alive! Thus, our plight is that for all humanity—sin is ever-present at the door. We who are connected to both divinity and humanity must stand ever assiduous in guarding the gates of our souls.

Sin the Supreme Separator

On becoming aware of the deceitful and undermining tactics of the federal government to systematically subvert the gains and growing unity among civil rights organizations, or more recently, the destruction of the Black Panther Party for Self Defense, the attack on the Young Lord's, and the instigation of the Bloods and Crips through mysterious donations of armaments and agitation, I was nothing short of livid! I can remember stomping into the living room of my parent's home and launching into one of my tirades about this country's fascination and love of racism and oppression. After a few minutes of my private rebuke, my father simply suggested that the fascination is not about racism, exploitation, or oppression, "It's a sin issue! All those things are a byproduct of the condition of a person's heart. When a person or government loves sin, then such is the result." Although I wanted to focus on a more esoteric systemic demon, I had to start with understanding that governments are comprised of people, and it is the people who are bent on forming systems that promote their sinful heart's agenda. Because sin is a spiritual malaise, a personal entanglement, and a mysterious magnetic downward pulling to overshadow our God consciousness, the only answer to be found is in the Gospel of Jesus. The Church is the most qualified agent of hope to combat the sins of this world.

The connected consciousness of the pavement preacher witnesses firsthand the struggles of the masses, the sickness of sin in the oppressors, and brings to ministry a certain sense of soberness. Let us remember that bitterness, resentment, hatred, and revenge constitute a deadly cocktail that all men and women are tempted to partake of. The pavement minister must remain acutely aware of this temptation and continually resort to critical self-introspection, in order to eradicate such cancerous diseases of the soul. Thus, we find that our assignment to address the root of racism, classicism, and oppression really culminates in eliminating a small three-letter word, sin. This is not to suggest that one ignore the systemic implications that exist from the continued nurturing of sin, because these implications require the immediacy of our attention and action. The intent for presenting the issue of sin is to suggest that no philosophical, ideological, psychological construct or plan to reverse the dire predicament of our people will be successful if devoid of the spiritual infusion of dealing with the souls of people. Since, our departure from the intended course of harmonious coexistence of humanity, the Church has no other choice, but to work with and among those most affected by the world's global indulgence in sin. Our continual prayer is to embrace the Eastern Christian concept, theosis, the continual and constant human endeavor to be one with God and humanity.

CHAPTER 11

THE MINISTRY OF MALCOLM X

"And other sheep I have, which are not of this fold: them also I must bring, and they shall hear my voice; and there shall be one fold, and one shepherd."

—John 10:16

The Ministry of Malcolm X: Moving Beyond the Hype

Perhaps the genius or gifting of Malcolm X has slipped through the quivering theological fingers of the black church. Black Christians were unable to fully grasp Malcolm in his lifetime, and I dare say, we continue to struggle with his complex identity today. Maybe it is due to Malcolm's venomous strikes at black clergy or perhaps it is because of his polarizing message of black withdrawal from all things American. Whether it is for one or the other, it has led us to distance ourselves from his legacy. However, transcending all the things that drove a wedge between Malcolm and the masses was his ability to tell it like it is. This was a dangerous quality for anyone to possess, let alone follow. Although he was a devout adherent of Islam, early on filtered through the Nation of Islam and the teaching of Elijah Muhammad, he had a love for black people that defied political correctness. Although I am an authentic and committed Christian for life, I am most attracted to the unifying message of black solidarity that was presented by this fiery pavement preacher.

This one-time, so-called Black Muslim held the office of national minister of the Nation of Islam. A former street hustler and convicted felon, he became attracted to the teachings of the Honorable Elijah Muhammad as an alternative to Christianity, which, according to the Nation of Islam, was the perfect slave-making religion. Because Malcolm and his family were the victims of malicious attacks by whites, it was not a far stretch for him to believe that all whites were deceitful "blue-eyed devils." Malcolm's zeal was second to none. He preached, taught, lectured, organized, and worked diligently, starting new mosques in the northern states, and declaring that blacks had the right like any other ethnic group, to defend themselves from white violence. Unfortunately, blacks and whites labeled him a violent lunatic, existing on the fringe of social change.

In time, internal jealously, the revelation of the moral failure of Elijah Muhammad, and differing views for the direction of the Nation of Islam forced Malcolm out. The departure allowed Malcolm to develop a new organization that would have a much broader scope and agenda. While Malcolm was a member of the Nation, he was restricted in his efforts to work in the civil rights movement, which became one of his intents during his last year in the Nation of Islam. There, his work was solely religious in nature and his ideology was separatist. But as the leader of the Organization of Afro-American Unity, he returned to a more orthodox Islamic belief, as a foundation upon which to build Afro-American unity, to break down the barriers of separatist ideals, and to distance himself from the non-political involvement in the electoral politics ideology of the Nation of Islam.

Malcolm's departure from the Nation of Islam resulted in a gradual acceptance of the work of black Christians involved in the civil rights movement and a greater understanding of whites, as well as an admittance of the sweeping indictments he often made, coming to these realizations in his last year of life. Malcolm was assassinated at a time when he was endeavoring to connect the twenty-two million Afro-Americans in the United States to the millions of black and brown people in the world. In his eyes, blacks in America were not a minority, but part of a worldwide majority. Through this majority, he would push the civil rights movement into the sphere of human rights, with intentions to bring the United States before the world court of the United Nations. He stood in solidarity with the disenfranchised everywhere, always seeing himself as part of the rejected masses, despite any level of earned respect that he acquired from whites or middle-class blacks.

Malcolm presented a model of pavement ministry that shook the people-pleasing conservative blacks and paternalistic whites to the core, forcing upon them a realization of the depths of black suffering without pretense. His ministry and his words were nothing short of what I call a *guerilla gospel*—a method of moving in unconventional ways that shatter the operational modes of the traditional methodologies of preachers to reach the lost. He understood the pathology of poor communities and the predatory exploitation, taking place in black communities. He was a student of the ebb and flow of street movement; that is to say, he was acutely aware of how the masses and the criminal underworld of black culture thought and moved, because he was one of them. Malcolm knew that the oppressed masses were not in the least interested in black preacher appropriations of Western philosophy, middle classness, or education. What intrigued the masses was a sense of realism— the perceived authenticity of a person speaking on their behalf. Although many considered him a demagogue and his speech divisive, he nonetheless possessed the courage to publically confront the reality of unyielding white supremacy.

The pedagogy of the streets is intrinsically germane to change, and Malcolm X possessed it fully. He had the richness of realism. He utilized moral strength to remove the mask that the black middle class and the church of his day frequently wore. He had the ability to stand in the solitude of being, with such equanimity of mind and soul that the environment was forced to acknowledge that realness. The ethos of Malcolm X was, not to simply serve the oppressed, but also to liberate black people. He was uninterested in demonstrations or dialogues with oppressive agents. Malcolm possessed the urgency of the biblical prophet Moses, demanding the immediate termination of slavery. He understood that with respect to dialogue, both parties must be equally respected and considered. Thus, until blacks are afforded the human right of being treated equal, dialogue cannot exist, only a demand for freedom. Malcolm's militancy and pugilistic posture were an effort to say to America in so many words, you have slavery in your blood, and your very thoughts are oppressive. It was his blatant and bold declaration of America's false foundation of freedom that led him to say:

"No, I'm not an American. I am one of twenty-two million black people, who are the victims of Americanism. One of the... victims of democracy, nothing but disguised hypocrisy. So, I'm not standing here speaking to you as an American, or a patriot, or a flag-saluter, or a flag-waver—no, not I! I'm speaking as a victim of this American system. And I see America through the eyes of the victim. I don't see any American dream; I see an American nightmare."[83]

The nightmare was filled with the horror of living in a society that consistently devalued and diminished blacks, a nightmare that could only be dispelled by pavement ministry.

The Value of All Black Life

There is a famous quote often repeated from John Singleton's motion picture, *Boyz N the Hood.* Doughboy, played by actor and rapper Ice Cube, states after the murder of his brother by a rival gang, that there was no mention of the violent act on the news, and he ultimately concluded that, "either they don't know, don't show, or don't care about what's going on in the hood." Doughboy's quote highlights the fact that there is little difference in the result of intentional or unintentional indifference; the end result is a lingering lack of concern for the life of others.

A perfect example is the truncated pro-life argument. I truly believe that if opponents of abortion, of which I am one, would commit resources of time, money, and intelligent forethought in crafting arguments of a pro-life agenda that extends beyond the killing of unborn babies, we would be more successful. The broadening of the scope would considerably increase effectiveness in the public square. My challenge to the majority of the pro-life community is to become equally passionate about life after the child is born. Should not Head Start programs receive funding to ensure that the life so stringently fought for in the womb is able to receive the needed instruction that this program offers? Should not we advocate for adequate funding for poor children, who are confined to inadequate schools? I have heard no mention of overwhelming disgust with the fact that nine million of the children, for whom we fought to ensure birth, have no healthcare. Should not we urge more adoption of those babies, who, having been born, are homeless and/or unwanted? And are not the lives of women, who have been ensnared in the sex trade, as well as the lives of those who are incarcerated equally precious? Answering these questions in the affirmative will do much to broaden the scope of pro-life beyond the womb and extend it to the grave.

I believe the mission of the Church should involve the preservation of the sanctity of all life, not just the neatly-packaged, pristine, all-American ideal of perfection. Likewise, I find it equally appalling for black churches to march, seek press time, and stir every resident to action, in the case of white violence inflicted upon black life, only to be found missing in action when that violence becomes black-on-black. Life is a gift, and the hope that fuels the pavement preacher is the power of the Gospel to transform life into something meaningful and good. This was Malcolm's gift to us.

Malcolm saw the best in black life. This is why he made the prisons, dives, and dens his stomping grounds, searching out what others refused to see—that black life is valuable and should not be discarded. Men and women should not be seen as useless rubbish. Rather, one should commit one's life to rescuing people from the "trash heaps" of life, in order to restore the rejected. Malcolm, having been surrounded in his childhood by the hatred of whites in Omaha and Lansing, would later practically self-destruct in what he called the "Technicolor Bizarre" of the underworld economy, as he became involved in using and selling drugs, pimping, and stealing in Boston and New York. Ultimately, he was redeemed behind prison bars, making of his life a challenge for us to reach out to those who are most alienated by society and stand in solidarity with those who are oppressed. Malcolm's life is a testimony to the fact that redemption is truly possible.

CHAPTER 12

FOR REDEMPTION'S SAkE

*"For the grace of God that bringeth salvation hath appeared
to all men, Teaching us that, denying ungodliness and
worldly lusts, we should live soberly, righteously, and godly,
in this present world; Looking for that blessed hope, and the
glorious appearing of the great God and our Saviour Jesus
Christ; Who gave himself for us, that he might redeem us
from all iniquity, and purify unto himself a peculiar people,
zealous of good works."*

—Titus 2:11-14

For Redemption's Sake

The pavement preacher, who is committed to the principle
of solidarity, searches for ways to redeem the lost. I believe that
the black church and America may have missed an opportunity
to promote such. On December 13, 2005, Stanley Tookie
Williams was executed in California for the murders of two
convenience store workers. The case was highly controversial,

and the line was drawn in the sand with the undecided regulated to silence, as only the courageous opponents and proponents spoke. Despite the attempts of several high-profile stars and celebrities, like Snoop, Jamie Foxx, who also played Tookie in the motion picture "Redemption," Ed Asner, and many others, Tookie was nonetheless executed by lethal injection. The case involved a multiplicity of dimensions that included arguments of whether or not he was innocent of the murders or, at the very least, given a fair trial.

The black community has long understood that history is replete with wrongful convictions and executions of African-Americans. Atrocities, ranging from the Scottsboro Boys to the burning of Rosewood, are still a haunting memory. Moreover, the constant flow of overturned verdicts of wrongfully convicted black men attests to the many failures of the criminal justice system. Certainly, most errors can be charged to the politics of the death penalty, or the so-called war on crime and drugs, which turned out to be a war on black and brown people. Additionally, responsibility can be placed on those who strategically, during election seasons, throw into juxtaposition fear of escalating crime in our midst, the exigencies of an overburdened criminal justice system, and the ever-present volleying for political gain by both sides, prosecutorial and defense.

Writing these last few pages has caused me to reflect on my own evolution, concerning the death penalty. As a former Marine, Gulf War veteran, and juvenile boot camp drill instructor, I have from time to time held different views about the death penalty. After much soul searching and research, I must admit that blacks are more likely than other ethnic groups to receive sentences of capital punishment. Perhaps, it is a case of not having enough "capital" to offset the punishment. Furthermore, the findings of wrongful deaths and convictions, the moratorium on the death penalty in Illinois, and witnessing an increasing number of states waking to systemic racism have deeply informed my concerns about the death penalty. I vividly remember having a conversation with a black police chief about the discrepancies in sentencing, and he replied, "You won't necessarily go to jail because you are black, but you will definitely stay there longer because you are black." Still, in light of the overwhelming crisis associated with black incarceration and the possibility of redemptive action being a prerequisite for confronting and adjusting what passes for normal in the contemporary justice system, some definitive action must soon take place. This provides a great opportunity for the church to make known to all that God seeks to save the lost. Some immediate actions come readily to mind. First, the black church should lobby for a national moratorium on the death penalty, especially in those cases where DNA has either not been allowed or is unavailable. Secondly, the church must present a more inclusive definition and historical review of "violent gangs" in America, so that a contextual framework may be provided as a point of reference, to begin discussion about violence among our youth.

America: It's All Gangster!

This country has had a romantic relationship with gangsters, whether it is the tailor-suited mobsters or the flannel-shirted and rag-attired homies. It's all gangster! Opponents of Stanley Tookie Williams' appeal for life protested that even if he were innocent of the murder charges, he started a gang that caused innumerable deaths. Thus, the death penalty was justified or, at the very least, indifference toward his case was definitely warranted. In the same vein, there is no question that the Crips are indeed a deadly and notorious gang. However, if gang involvement is the issue, what says history? In 1926, mob boss Al Capone was arrested for killing three people, but the gangster spent only one night in jail because of a lack of evidence. Three years later, in May of 1929, Capone served his first prison sentence; however, it was not for murder, but for a misdemeanor of simply carrying a gun. A year later, at the height of his thuggish reign, Capone rose to the top of Chicago's list of the twenty-eight worst criminals, and was considered the city's "Public Enemy Number One." In 1931, Capone was finally indicted for income tax evasion. He was sentenced to a total of ten years in federal prison and one year in the county jail.

Additionally, opponents argued that Tookie remained in control of the Crips and was directly responsible for the gang's direction while incarcerated. The argument is valid and positional leadership has far-reaching influence. But before we draw conclusions in haste, let us consider Capone again. Much the same, in May 1932, Capone was sent to the harshest federal prison at that time in Atlanta, GA. While imprisoned, it was common knowledge that Capone organized, facilitated, and directed his mob organization from inside the prison. The record reveals that, while incarcerated in Atlanta, Capone secured extravagant privileges and cell furnishing, like a typewriter, rugs, and a set of the Encyclopedia Britannica. Let us be mindful that Capone was able to secure such conveniences in the toughest of federal prisons. One can only imagine what other privileges he was granted. Al Capone was sent to Alcatraz to finish his sentence. In 1938, he was transferred to Terminal Island Prison in California and released in 1939. Capone, by all accounts, manipulated his surroundings in Atlanta, and escaped severe punishment, as it pertains to his crimes. History reminds us that it is possible that punishment is less about what you do, as it is dependant upon who you are and the status of your financial holdings.

If the historical analogy is not enough, consider Gotti. John was a known killer, who, with the help of his attorney Roy Cone, was able to successfully avoid the death penalty and receive life in prison. In light of this, his family was rewarded with a reality show, *"Growing up Gotti,"* on A&E. Instead of shame, it was fame. How soon we forget or acquire selective amnesia. Neither Capone nor Gotti contributed to anything notable in the realm of reconciling the damage they enacted upon the community and their families. Yet, neither received the death penalty. In contrast, Tookie worked very hard to de-romanticize gang life and gang culture, while America continues its schizophrenic fascination with gangsterism. Consider gangster rap (if you use that descriptive clause) that continues to be bought in the largest quantities by white youth. The past and present pop culture have an insatiable appetite for gangsterism as motion pictures like *The Godfather, Scarface,* and *Goodfellas,* are celebrated, and sitcoms like the *Sopranos,* attract many faithful viewers each week. The larger society often abhors the expressions of gangsterism portrayed in black pigment, while it romanticizes it in lighter hue in film, and overlooks it in reality. For me, redemption signifies a life turned around. It is an act of mercy, bestowed on behalf of the guilty. Although Stanley never admitted being guilty of the murders, he did confess guilt to his past life of violence and damage. He was not, by any stretch of the imagination, a man free of his past actions. I do believe, however, that he could have rendered additional acts of redemption, if allowed to live, by ministering to countless youth caught in a vicious cycle of like violence. Tookie's redemption caused one-time rival gang members from the "Bloods" to intercede on his behalf. In a plea for his life, in good faith, they turned assault weapons over to the police, which were taken off the streets through the agency of Black Entertainment Television (BET). They further vowed to help remove additional guns off the streets if Stanley's life was spared. What a lost opportunity for the church, the community, and the criminal justice system. Nonetheless, Stanley's demise, youth violence, and redemption provide much food for thought.

First and foremost, at the time of Stanley's conviction, he was a gang member. The fact of his gang involvement challenges the black church to confront the violence being perpetrated by black boys, and now by an even faster growing populace of young black women. The challenge of gangs is massive. Unfortunately, churches do not address or frame a meaningful dialogue about violence in general, i.e., domestic abuse, child abuse, and spousal rape, not to mention gang violence, until confronted with shootings, stabbings, or funerals. We must strategize, become proactive, and develop methods of providing a safe sanctuary for victims to share, and aggressively build partnerships to relieve communities of the disruptive violence, while seeking to redeem as many proponents of these acts as possible.

Next, "Redemption" is not just secular, it is a theological word with foundation in both the Old and New Testaments. The church must provide clarity when the public square becomes attached to language that has historical and spiritual roots. I know of no other institution that can provide the kind of defining understanding proclaimed by the church, because we have firsthand knowledge of what it means to be "redeemed." Finally, the church should address the plethora of murders committed by black and Latino youth. The church must define its implications and detail its ramifications on the total community. We must address the psychological imprint and the soul-scarring forced upon youth, who are already alienated politically, socially, and yes, even spiritually. It is our responsibility to abate the unbalanced message of retribution without redemption that society continues to send.

The case of Stanley Williams is not to be taken as a personal diatribe about the racist criminal justice system. Rather, it should serve to encourage critical thinking in the exploration of methodologies of protest and prevention, while developing strategic alternatives to this current gang and prison culture. The fear is that we will indeed continue to miss opportunities to engage the current youth culture. Can the church afford to stand back and listen only to major cable network channels and the local nightly news, as they spotlight, with striking imagery, shackled, orange jump-suited, and flip-flop wearing black males, being carted off like cattle? Is there not some disconnect between their prevailing images of crime, while BET blissfully broadcasts crime-glorifying videos and music? I greatly appreciated the valiant efforts made by Rev. Al Sharpton, Rev. Jesse Jackson, and Bruce Gordon, the former President of the NAACP, in an attempt to bring intellectual, rational, political, and theological significance to the case of Stanley Tookie Williams. Although in retrospect, I am convinced that a unified local grassroots effort, inclusive of engaged black churches throughout America, would have sent a message that redemption from the death penalty, not freedom from jail, is more desirable than retribution. Only those who have been guilty and recognize their many offenses can properly promote redemption, as God offers salvation also to the offender. As Christians, we know that our sins, failings, and faults are but a brief memory away.

Power on the Pavement

The issue of youth and gang violence is a cancer of the worst magnitude. I believe the black church as a collective body has been far too quiet on the issue of violence, period. Particularly in the larger, more sophisticated churches, I make note that the sophistication is not found in the intelligence of the membership, but in the technology and resources of middle-class blacks. It appears that it is the smaller or storefront, independent, charismatic or Pentecostal persuasion churches that have done noteworthy and traceable work among violent youth. There may be several reasons for this assertion.

First, the Pentecostal church in its early days was a rejected church. Its membership was primarily poor and uneducated. The code of conduct of these churches included clothing and dress regulations, and an overall refusal to be part of the secular "world." All served to polarize the church, leaving it on the fringes of Christianity in America. Perhaps, being accustomed to rejection or being viewed as outsiders has helped them to reach individuals, who are considered outsiders in other ways. One thing is for sure, Pentecostals possess a belief that one's acceptance of Jesus and the indwelling of the Holy Spirit make one a prime candidate for transformation. Thus, the outcast has a place of consistent, nurturing, and healing environment in which to become a renewed person.

Secondly, the location of these churches in urban and troubled areas is of great significance. The proximity to the predicament provides opportunity for possible God encounters. People scoff and scorn churches on every corner, but the very fact that they are present enhances the possibility for redemption. Finally, having evening services, scheduled and frequent prayer sessions, and additional events at the church provide residents of the community with alternative activities for additional support and guidance. Of course, research is needed to validate these presuppositions. They simply arise out of my personal experiences in storefronts. Significantly, with limited resources and meager facilities, these churches help repair the damage of neglect, dependency, and poverty. However, let me be painfully clear. This does not mean that all storefront or small churches are effective in these endeavors, nor does it mean that larger churches are not similarly and effectively involved in pavement ministry. It simply means that the smaller, more intimate churches seem to engage in this type of ministry more frequently.

After all, the size and location of a church does not necessarily have to be the determining factor in the type of service being rendered. Any church can become indifferent and cold to the surrounding youth, unless active intervention through the leadership of the pastor and engagement of the congregation invoke more compassionate direction via pavement ministry. By no means, do I postulate that churches confront the issue of violence from the pulpit with directive discourse that is intended solely for youth outside the walls. Indeed not, for the challenge of youth violence requires that urban and suburban, large and small, traditional or contemporary —all unite in valuing black life enough to break the silence of indifference, and move proactively in lockstep to promote ministry through informed pavement preachers.

Be mindful of the fact that the complicated and complex issue of youth violence cannot be undertaken without examining the failure of the church to pursue vigorously the need for a robust prison ministry. It is not only unbiblical, but a blatant sin to overlook this ministry. If we are in fact followers of Jesus, then we must look at the model left to us by our exemplar, found in Luke 4:18 -19. The Gospel writer Luke and the prophet Isaiah, in Isaiah 61, challenges us to indeed, "set the captives free." This mandate includes release from the physical, social, and spiritual prisons of the day. The church must respond as advocates for those who have received harsh and distorted sentences, due to minor infractions that warrant reversal or reconsideration. Why should the black church commit to service in the realm of prison ministry? If we use the case of Stanley Williams, we must be honest and cite that his prison transformation was rare. Like Malcolm, it was by the grace of God that Williams was able to make serious and lasting changes in his behavior behind bars. However, in truth, there are black men and women who will need additional assistance in making transformative decisions. There is no doubt that churches can do much more to assist in breaking apart the spiritual and mental chains of negative behavior.

With this in mind, why do not more churches get involved in this ministry? The answer is simple: Prison ministry is not in vogue. Preachers are neither privy to, nor allowed to collect offerings in prison, nor can their personal products be sold. Usually, there will be no television crews or video cameras, or need for sermons solely rooted in the prosperity gospel. Peddlers of the money-only messages will not have inmates swinging from the rafters. Admittedly, everyone in the local church cannot go into the jails, but prison ministry can be defined more broadly than prison visitation, although that is sorely needed.

Whether we respond or not, prison ministry is one of the dire needs that should be met by the church. When we consider that one out of three black men are currently or will be enmeshed in the criminal justice system, a fact that has a great detrimental impact on the culture, we must respond. In America, the prison culture, although behind the scenes, drives much of what we consider to be urban culture, language, music, dress, and contributes to political disenfranchisement, as felony convictions prohibit a set population from full citizenship. Prison continues to plague society by the fracturing of families, as incarcerated fathers and mothers are forced to raise their children through collect calls and letters. Additionally, prison sex, which in some estimates involves 40 percent of male populations on the conservative end, and the known rape culture directly contribute to the ever-growing statistics of black women who are contracting the deadly virus of HIV and AIDS. If the black Church does not make a focused and consistent effort to shatter the "jail trail," and address the social conditions that feed it, we will be forced into a war where the enemy is us!

EPILOGUE

A SAVING HOPE

*"According to my earnest expectation and my **hope**, that in nothing I shall be ashamed, but that with all boldness, as always, so now also Christ shall be magnified in my body, whether it be by life, or by death."*

—*Philippians 1:20*

We must demonstrate, teach, and preach, until the very foundations of our nation are shaken.

Martin Luther king, Jr.

"The day we see the truth and cease to speak is the day we begin to die."

—Dr. Martin Luther King, Jr.

There comes a time in the life of those who are dearly concerned about the Church and its role in the public square to articulate a call to action. As you may expect, there is no easy way or tried or true pattern to be used in calling institutions and people to action. Furthermore, such a challenge always denotes a certain level of healthy self-critique, wherein I have, at times, spoken critically about the black church and preacher in a universal sense. I hope to have done so lovingly, with the expectation that collectively, we will rise to a higher standard of service to God and humanity. It takes considerable effort and courage to discern our responsibility, as citizens of Heaven and earth, to move the church—the living brick and mortar of the kingdom of God—to collective action.

Perhaps our greatest challenge is overcoming the division and separatism that threatens the church. Sadly, the universal church is divided by our denominations and what I refer to as our "house rules"—the regulations of individual worship centers that have little to do with salvation. These rules focus more on precepts of localized understandings of sanctification. In saying such, let it be known that I appreciate our denominations and their histories. However, if we worship our denomination over our Christ, we will always stand divided. In other words, we all have observances and beliefs that are perceived as being pleasing to the Father, like order of worship, baptism rites, and understandings of Holy Communion. Such issues are vitally important to the fellowship of believers, who worship at your particular location. But when these individual "house rules" are brought to the universal church, they force believers to stand as opponents, rather than as allies. Jesus alone unifies us. His blood pardoned our sins and His death and resurrection justify us. We are in fact, one!

The work that we are called to embark upon requires that we work together and see ourselves as an interdependent whole, where disagreeing viewpoints are a part of coexistence.

Thus, let us follow suit with king, as he often quoted John Donne's famous poem, "No man is an island entire of itself. Every man is a piece of the continent, a part of the main...Any man's death diminishes me because I am involved in mankind; therefore never send to know for whom the bells tolls; it tolls for thee."[84] The preacher must see himself or herself as a part of the world, divinely called to make the world a better place, but nonetheless a part of it. We are inordinately involved in the good and the bad, the notable and the obscure. We are both the scientist and the experiment, privy to all the flaws in America's so-called democracy.

This book has been a labor of love for me. I have truthfully exposed the core principles that have directed my life. I am a Christian, shaped by the African experience in America. I pray that my experience and service have produced an earned influence to respectfully say that which I cannot deny. Because of my intimate relationship with the Church, this book is not rendered as the research of an outsider anthropologist or participant observer, but one who is committed to the advancement of the kingdom of God, along with the edification of the black community and the world at large. Let us embrace the best in black church pulpiteers, platform, and pavement preachers, who have labored to save the masses and died in the hope that the next generation would take up the mandate and mantel to offer salvation to a lost world. Let us rise with an invigorated sense of renewed hope—an expectation not manufactured in happiness or prosperity, but one that arises out of the ashes and is generated in the face of insurmountable odds. Let us continue to work for the spiritual and social renewal of the world. Let our service remain a labor of love that is *"Never Easy...Always Necessary!"*

NOTES

Introduction

[1] Robert M. Franklin, *Another Day's Journey: Black Churches Confronting the American Crisis* (Minneapolis: Fortress Press; 1997), p. 34.
[2] John 1:14
[1] Mark Lewis Taylor, *The Executed God: The Way of the Cross in Lockdown America* (Minneapolis: Fortress Press 2001), p. 57.
[2] Taylor, p. 57.

Chapter 1

[3] 2 Corinthians 5:17
[4] Galatians 5:1
[5] I use the term "Negro" purposefully for I believe that the "Black" church is what king helped to develop and is a result of the established theology of the Negro church, although, I will use the term "black" church for general references.
[6] W.E. Burghardt Dubois, *Souls of Black Folk* (New York: Signet Classic, 1995), p. 213.
[7] Lawrence N. Jones, "The Black Churches: A New Agenda," www. religion-online.org/cgi-bin.

[8] Dubois, *Souls of Black Folk*, p. 211.

[9] Ronald F. Thiemann, *Religion in Public Life: A Dilemma for Democracy* (Washington D.C.: Georgetown University Press, 1996), p. 151.

[10] Christopher H. Evans, *The Kingdom is Always Coming: A Life of Walter Rauschenbusch* (Grand Rapids: William B. Eerdmans Publishing Company, 2004), p. 179.

[11] Darryl M. Trimiew, "The Social Gospel Movement and the Question of Race," *The Social Gospel Today*, ed. Christopher H. Evans (Louisville: Westminster John knox Press, 2001), p. 27.

[12] Evans, *The Kingdom*, p. 179.

[13] Trimiew, *The Social Gospel*, p. 27.

[14] Evans, *The Kingdom*, p. 255.

Chapter 2

[15] Gardner C. Taylor, *The Words of Gardner C. Taylor: Lectures, Essays, and Interviews*, Vol. 5, ed. Edward L. Taylor (Valley Forge: Judson Press, 2001), p. 160.

[16] 2 Corinthians 5:21

[17] Isaiah 53:4

[18] Hebrews 4:15

Chapter 3

[19] St. John 3:17

[20] St. John 1:29

[21] St. John 3:30

[22] Hebrews 4:15

[23] Acts 4:13

[24] Acts 4:12

Chapter 4

[25] 2 Corinthians 6:17
[26] St. John 8:36
[27] Philippians 4:13
[28] 1 Corinthians 14:34-35
[29] Galatians 3:28

Chapter 5

[30] St. Matthew 6:10
[31] 2 Corinthians 5:17
[32] Ephesians 5:23

Chapter 6

[33] 1 Timothy 5:18
[34] Franklin, *Another's Day Journey*, p. 58.
[35] St. Luke 19:10
[36] Franklin, *Another Day's Journey*, p. 34.
[37] king, *A Testament*, p. 282.
[38] king, "Southern Christian."

Chapter 7

[39] Janet Marsden, review of *The Paradoxical Vision: A Public Theology for the Twenty-first Century,* by Robert Benne, www.firstthings.com/ ft9506/reviews/marsden.html.
[40] king, "Southern Christian."
[41] king, *A Testament*, p. 282.
[42] The concept of "political goods" were initially derived from Dr. Robert M. Franklin lectures, "The Art of Black Preaching, Harvard Divinity School 2002.
[43] Matthew 5:44

[44] Amos 5:24

[45] king, *A Testament*, p. 297.

[46] Molefi k. Asante, *The Afrocentric Idea* (Philadelphia: Temple University Press, 1998), p. 139.

[47] king, *A Testament*, p. 140.

[48] king, *A Testament*, p. 270.

Chapter 8

[49] Martin Luther king, Jr., *A Knock at Midnight, Inspiration from the Great Sermons of Reverend Martin Luther King, Jr.*, ed. Clayborne Carson and Peter Holloran (New York: Warner Books, Inc; 2000), p. 146.

[50] James H. Cone, *Martin and Malcolm and America: A Dream or a Nightmare* (Maryknoll, NY: Orbis Books, 1991), p. 123.

[51] Romans 10:17

[52] Martin Luther king, Jr., *The Autobiography of Martin Luther King, Jr.*, ed. Clayborne Carson (New York: Warner Books, Inc., 1998), p. 11.

[53] king, *The Autobiography*, p. 15.

[54] Martin Luther king, Jr., *A Testament of Hope: The Essential Writings and Speeches of Martin Luther King, Jr.*, ed. James M. Washington (New York: HarperCollins Publishers, 1991), p. ix.

[55] king, *Testament*, p. 345.

[56] Christopher H. Evans, *The Kingdom is Always Coming: A Life of Walter Rauschenbusch* (Grand Rapids: William B. Eerdmans Publishing Company, 2004), p. 179.

[57] Darryl M. Trimiew, "The Social Gospel Movement and the Question of Race," *The Social Gospel Today*, ed. Christopher H. Evans (Louisville: Westminster John knox Press, 2001), p. 27.

[58] Trimiew, *The Social Gospel*, p. 35.

[59] Trimiew, *The Social Gospel*, p. 29.

[60] Trimiew, *The Social Gospel*, p. 29.

Chapter 9

[61] The norms were derived from Professor Ronald Thiemann, Harvard Divinity School; Religion in the Public Square, Spring 2004 class lectures.
[62] king, *A Testament of Hope*, p. 220.
[63] king, *A Testament of Hope*, p. 220.
[64] Thiemann, Ronald Religion in Public Life p170
[65] Martin Luther king, Jr., *Why We Can't Wait* (New York: Signet Classic, 2000), p. 70.
[66] king, *Knock at Midnight*, p. 221.
[67] king, *Knock at Midnight*, p. 132.
[68] Thiemann, Religion in Public, p. 151.
[69] Acts 2:46-47.
[70]Marsden, *Review*.

Chapter 10

[71] Stewart Burns, *To The Mountain Top: Martin Luther King Jr.'s Sacred Mission To Save America 1955 – 1968* (New York: HarperSanFrancisco, 2004), p. 56.
[72] "Daddy king" was the term of endearment for the senior king, Martin's father.
[73] Martin Luther king Jr., *Stride Toward Freedom* (New York: Harper
& Row, 1958), p. 145.
[74] Burns, *To The Mountain*.
[75] Cone, *Martin and Malcolm*, p. 223.
[76] Ezekiel 3:15
[77] Leland and kalb, "Savior."
[78] J. H. O'Dell, "Life in Mississippi: An Interview with Fannie Lou Hamer, No.2, 1965," *The Freedom Ways Reader: Prophets in*

Their Own Country, ed. Esther Cooper Jackson and Constance Pohl (Boulder: Westview Press, 2000) p. 99.
79

[80] Genesis 2:7

Chapter 11

[81] Comments rendered by Malcolm X at Cory Methodist Church, Cleveland Ohio, April 3, 1964.

Epilogue

[82] king, *A Knock*, p. 208.

BIBLIOGRAPHY

Asante, Molefi k. *The Afrocentric Idea.* Philadelphia: Temple University Press, 1998.

Boulton, Wayne G. *From Christ to the World, Introductory Readings in Christian Ethics: An Introduction to Christian Ethics*, Eds. Wayne G. Boulton, Thomas D. kennedy and Allen Verhey. Grand Rapids: William B. Eerdmans Publishing Company, 1994.

Burns, Stewart. *Daybreak of Freedom.* Chapel Hill: University of North Carolina Press, 1997.

Cone, James H. *Martin and Malcolm and America: A Dream or a Nightmare.* Maryknoll, NY: Orbis Books, 1991.

Burns, Stewart. *To The Mountain Top: Martin Luther King Jr.'s Sacred Mission To Save America 1955 – 1968.* New York: HarperSanFrancisco, 2004.

Du Bois, W.E. Burghardt. *The Souls of Black Folk.* First published 1903, Everyman's Library, Alfred A. knopf, New York, Toronto 1993.

Evans, Christopher H. *The Kingdom is Always Coming: A life of Walter Rauschenbusch.* Grand Rapids: William B. Eerdmans Publishing Company, 2004.

Franklin, Robert M. *Another Day's Journey: Black Churches Confronting the American Crisis.* Minneapolis: Fortress Press, 1997.

king Jr., Martin Luther. *A Knock at Midnight, Inspiration from the Great Sermons of Reverend Martin Luther King, Jr.* Ed. Clayborne Carson and Peter Hollerman. New York: Warner Books, Inc., 2000.

king Jr., Martin Luther. *A Testament of Hope: The Essential Writings and Speeches of Martin Luther King, Jr.* Ed. James

M. Washington. New York: HarperCollins Publishers, 1991.

King Jr., Martin Luther. *Stride Toward Freedom.* New York: Harper & Row, 1958. King Jr., Martin Luther. *The Autobiography of Martin Luther King, Jr.* Ed. Carson Clayborne. New York: Warner Books, Inc., 1998.

Taylor, Gardner C. *The Words of Gardner C. Taylor, Lectures, Essays, and Interviews*, vol 5, Ed. Edward L. Taylor. Valley Forge: Judson Press, 2001.

Taylor, Gardner C. *The Words of Gardner C. Taylor, Special Occasion and Expository Sermons*, vol 4, Ed. Edward L. Taylor. Valley Forge: Judson Press, 2001.

Taylor, Mark Lewis. *The Executed God: The Way of the Cross in Lockdown America.* Minneapolis: Fortress Press, 2001.

Thiemann, Ronald F. *Religion in Public Life: A Dilemma for Democracy.* Washington D.C.: Georgetown University Press, 1996.

Trimiew, Darryl M. *The Social Gospel Movement and the Question of Race: The Social Gospel Today.* Ed. Christopher H. Evans. Louisville: Westiminster John knox Press, 2001.

Washington, James Melvin. *Frustrated Fellowship: The Black Baptist Quest for Social Power.* Macon: Mercer, 1986.

Magazine Articles

Flynn, Sean. "The Hustler Prophet," *Boston Magazine*, December 1996.

Hodge, Sharon Brooks. "Rep. Floyd Flake," *Headway* 8, Jan 1996.

Richardson, Gwen Daye, Robert Stanton. "20 Most Influential Black Conservatives," *Headway* 8, September 1997.

Kalb, Claudia and Leland, John. "Savior of the Streets," *Newsweek*, 1 June 1998.

Parker, Anthony A. "In Jesus' Name: Azusa Christian Community Reclaims the Poor and Disposed in Boston," *Sojourners*, May 1993.

Interviews

Rivers III., Eugene F. "Word on the Street." Interview by C. Stephen Evans and Gail Gunst Heffner. www.christianitytoday.com/ct/2001/132/24.0.html.

Rivers, III., Eugene F. "Muddy River." Interview by Sandra Gregg. www.horizonmag.com/poverty/eugene-rivers.asp.

Flake, Floyd. "Religion and Ethics." *Newsweekly*. Episode 804. Interview by kelly Hudson. 24 September 2004.

John Leland with Claudia kalb. *Savior of the Streets*.

Newsweek. June 1, 1998.

Web Sources

Jones, Lawrence N. "The Black Churches: A New Agenda." www.religion-online.org/cgi-binwww.religion-online.org/cgi-bin.

Additional Resources

Class lecture presented by Dr. Ronald Thiemann on 10 March 2004 entitled Martin Luther king, Jr., as Public Theologian: *"Letter from Birmingham City Jail."*

king, Jr., Martin L. "Southern Christian Leadership Conference Speech at Staff Retreat," Penn Center, Frogmore South Carolina. Memorial Center in the Oral History Project, May 1967.

Marsden, Janet. Review of *The Paradoxical Vision: A Public Theology for the Twenty-first Century*. By Robert Benne. www.firstthings.com/ft9506/reviews/marsden.html.

ABOUT THE AUTHOR

Reverend Dwight Ford is an innovative leader, author, thought-provoker, and public theologian. He is affectionately known as "The People's Pastor," for his commitment to vulnerable populations and impoverished communities. His service to society is a seamless merging of the "theological why" with "a practical how." His life is a constant leap of faith across pulpits, platforms, and pavement as he endeavors to transform present-day realities into tomorrow's opportunities.

He was born in Crystal Springs, Mississippi and reared in Rock Island, Illinois. Upon graduating high school, he enlisted in the United States Marine Corps and successfully completed a six-year military career which included Operation Desert Shield and Operation Desert Storm service tours. He earned various awards and was listed in the top ten percent of enlisted Marines.

Reverend Ford holds a Bachelor of Arts degree from Western Illinois University, with a concentration in Business Management and Leadership. He also holds the Master of Divinity degree from Harvard University in Cambridge, MA. His research was centered on the Greek New Testament, Public Theology of the Civil Rights Era (1954 – 1968), Community Economic Development, and the agency of the African American Church. He was the winner of the esteemed Billings Preacher Award and served as the Program Coordinator for

Harvard Divinity School's Summer Leadership Institute, an intensive program to train pastors and leaders in community and economic development.

In his most recent positions, Rev. Ford served as the Executive Director of Eastern Nebraska Community Action Partnership in Omaha, Nebraska and The Martin Luther King Jr. Community Center in Rock Island, Illinois. Currently, he serves as Board Member to various local community organizations. He is a proud member of Alpha Phi Alpha Fraternity, Incorporated.

Reverend Ford is an ordained Baptist minister of the National Baptist Convention, USA, Inc., and has served in pastoral ministry for over 23 years. He is the founder and pastor of Grace City Church in Moline, Illinois. When Pastor Ford is not in his regular role in the pulpit of Grace City, he can be found traveling throughout the United States as a minister of the Gospel and public speaker to churches, colleges, and community organizations. He provides professional services of consultation for public schools and community partnerships, strategic planning and implementation strategy, church and community projects.

He is married to the former Argrow Kitnequa Evans and together they have a beautiful daughter Imani Argrow Ford. Reverend Ford has devoted his life to serving the church and underserved populations of the world. His passion to build self-sufficiency in impoverished communities can be summarized in his words, "poverty is indeed persistent. It's problematic in so many ways, but I chose to believe that poverty does not have to be permanent! Children born today in the socio-economic basement will be able to reside on the balcony of tomorrow's opportunity."

www.ingramcontent.com/pod-product-compliance
Lightning Source LLC
LaVergne TN
LVHW011231080426
835509LV00005B/445